SOCCER

Steps to Success

Second Edition

Joseph A. Luxbacher, PhD
University of Pittsburgh

Human Kinetics

Library of Congress Cataloging-in-Publication Data

Luxbacher, Joe
   Soccer : steps to success / by Joseph A. Luxbacher. — 2nd ed.
     p.   cm. -- (Steps to success activity series)
   ISBN 0-87322-763-8
    1. Soccer. I. Title. II. Series.
   GV943.L87   1995
   796.334'2--dc20

                                                    95-44483
                                                         CIP

ISBN: 0-87322-763-8

Human Kinetics books are available at special discounts for bulk purchase. Special editions or book excerpts can also be created to specification. For details, contact the Special Sales Manager at Human Kinetics.

Developmental Editor: Rodd Whelpley; **Assistant Editors:** Kent Reel, Sally Bayless; **Editorial Assistant:** Jennifer Hemphill; **Copyeditor:** June Waldman; **Proofreader:** Sally Bayless; **Typesetter:** Kathy Boudreau-Fuoss; **Text Designer:** Keith Blomberg; **Layout Artist:** Tara Welsch; **Cover Designer:** Jack Davis; **Photographer (cover):** Wilmer Zehr; **Illustrator:** Keith Blomberg; **MAC Illustrator:** Jennifer Delmotte; **Printer:** United Graphics

Instructional Designer for the Steps to Success Activity Series: Joan N. Vickers, EdD, University of Calgary, Calgary, Alberta, Canada

Printed in the United States of America   10   9   8   7   6   5   4   3

Human Kinetics
Web site: http://www.humankinetics.com/

United States: Human Kinetics, P.O. Box 5076, Champaign, IL 61825-5076
1-800-747-4457
e-mail: humank@hkusa.com

Canada: Human Kinetics, Box 24040, Windsor, ON N8Y 4Y9
1-800-465-7301 (in Canada only)
e-mail: humank@hkcanada.com

Europe: Human Kinetics, P.O. Box IW14, Leeds LS16 6TR, United Kingdom
(44) 1132 781708
e-mail: humank@hkeurope.com

Australia: Human Kinetics, 57A Price Avenue, Lower Mitcham, South Australia 5062
(088) 277 1555
e-mail: humank@hkaustralia.com

New Zealand: Human Kinetics, P.O. Box 105-231, Auckland 1
(09) 523 3462
e-mail: humank@hknewz.com

C ONTENTS

PREFACE

Soccer is the most popular sport on the planet. More than 200 million people worldwide play more than 20 million soccer games each year. To give you an idea of the magnitude of soccer's popularity, a television audience of more than 2 billion people watched Brazil defeat Italy in the 1994 World Cup final. Compare that figure to 750 million who watched the 1993 NFL Super Bowl, 350 million who watched the Wimbledon tennis final, and 490 million who watched the first man land on the moon.

The reasons for soccer's universal appeal rest with the nature of the game. Soccer is a game of physical and mental challenges. You must execute skilled movements under game-related conditions of restricted space, limited time, physical and mental fatigue, and opposing players. You must be able to run several miles during a game, mostly at sprintlike speed, and respond quickly to a variety of rapidly changing situations during play. Finally, you need a thorough understanding of individual, group, and team tactics. Your ability to meet all these challenges determines how well you perform on the soccer field.

Whether your orientation is purely recreational or highly competitive, you'll enjoy the game more as you master the skills and strategies required for successful play. The second edition of *Soccer: Steps to Success* provides a step-by-step plan for improving your soccer skills and developing a more complete understanding of tactics and strategies. The book is organized in a series of clearly defined steps that enable you to advance at your own pace. Illustrations clarify the proper execution of soccer skills and tactics, including those used by the goalkeeper. The drills at the end of each step begin with basic exercises and progress in complexity. The sequence of drills enables you to practice the fundamentals before you engage in game-simulated conditions. Once you have mastered the skills and tactics covered in one step, you are ready to move on to the next. At the end of your journey you will be ready to play the game of soccer.

Writing a book requires the support and cooperation of a great many people. I tip my hat to the outstanding, highly professional staff at Human Kinetics. Although I can't possibly mention all of the players by name, I would like to extend my sincere appreciation to the following individuals. To Judy Patterson Wright, my editor and friend, whose guidance and good humor helped to keep me on course when the writing was difficult; to Rodd Whelpley for his patience, persistence, and insight concerning revisions to the text; and to the many soccer coaches and players who were kind enough to share their knowledge and ideas. I would also like to thank my mom, Mary Ann Luxbacher, for her constant love and encouragement. Her support is steadfast in everything I do.

I especially want to express gratitude and love to my beautiful wife, Gail, the most special person in my life. Her willingness to sacrifice personal time for writing time when the deadlines drew near and to tolerate the moods and quirks of a sometimes frustrated author are deeply appreciated. Her constant love, support, and encouragement enabled me to complete this project.

THE STEPS TO SUCCESS STAIRCASE

Get ready to climb a staircase—one that will lead you to become an accomplished soccer player. You cannot leap to the top; you get there by climbing one step at a time. Each of the 10 steps you will take is an easy transition from the one before. The first few steps of the staircase provide a foundation of basic skills and concepts. As you progress further, you will learn how to connect groups of those seemingly isolated skills. You will learn how to consistently pass and receive the ball, how to shoot, and how to play individual offense and defense. As you near the top of the staircase, you will become more confident in your ability to play as a team member, both offensively and defensively, and you will learn how to communicate effectively with your teammates.

Familiarize yourself with this section, as well as the "Soccer: A World-Class Sport" section for an orientation and help in setting up your practice sessions around the steps. Follow the same sequence each step (chapter) of the way.

1. Read the explanations of what is covered in the step, why the step is important, and how to execute or perform the step's focus, which may be on basic skills, concepts, tactics, or a combination of the three.
2. Follow the numbered illustrations showing exactly how to position your body to execute each basic skill successfully. There are three general parts to each skill: preparation (getting into a starting position), execution (performing the skill that is the focus of the step), and follow-through (reaching a finish position or following through to starting position).
3. Look over the descriptions in the "Success Stoppers" section for common errors that may occur and the recommendations for how to correct them.
4. Read the directions and the Success Goals for each drill. Practice accordingly and record your scores. Compare your score with the Success Goals for the drill. You need to meet the Success Goals of each drill before moving on to practice the next one because the drills are arranged in an easy-to-difficult progression. This sequence is designed specifically to help you achieve continual success.
5. As soon as you can reach all the Success Goals for one step, you are ready for a qualified observer—such as your teacher, coach, or trained partner—to evaluate your basic skill technique against the Keys to Success items. This is an evaluation of your basic technique or form, which can enhance your performance.
6. Repeat these procedures for each of the 10 Steps to Success. Then rate yourself according to the directions in the "Rating Your Total Progress" section.

Good luck on your step-by-step journey to developing your soccer skills, building confidence, experiencing success, and having fun!

KEY

X = Offensive player

O = Defensive player

X⊕ = Player with the ball

– – ➤ = Path of the ball

——➤ = Path of player without the ball

∿∿➤ = Path of player dribbling the ball

S = Server

GK = Goalkeeper

SW = Sweeper back

STB = Stopper back

RB = Right back

LB = Left back

RMF = Right Midfielder

CMF = Center midfielder

LMF = Left midfielder

RFW = Right forward (winger)

LFW = Left forward (winger)

CS = Central striker (forward)

SOCCER: A WORLD-CLASS SPORT

S occer! The game evokes an outpouring of passion and emotion unparalleled within the realm of sport. Soccer is a common language among peoples of diverse backgrounds and heritages, a bridge that spans economic, political, cultural, and religious barriers. Known as "football" throughout most of the world, soccer is the national sport of nearly every country in Asia, Africa, Europe, and South America. It remains the only football-type game played at the Olympics. Millions more people follow the World Cup, soccer's international championship, than follow the Super Bowl and World Series. Soccer is without question the world's most popular game.

The Modern Game

In a global society divided by physical and ideological barriers, soccer's popularity is not restricted by age, sex, political, religious, cultural, or ethnic boundaries. The fluid, controlled movements of each player express his or her individuality within a team game. Speed, strength, stamina, skill, and tactical knowledge are all important aspects of performance. The variety of challenges confronting players may be the primary reason for the game's universal appeal.

The tactics of team play have undergone many modifications during the evolution of the sport. In the past players filled very specialized roles. Forwards were assigned the sole task of scoring goals, and defenders were expected to prevent the opposition from scoring. Positional responsibilities were narrowly defined, and there was little overlap of roles. Soccer today requires much more of players. The modern game places a premium on the complete soccer player, that is, the individual who can defend as well as attack. With the exception of the goalkeeper, the days of the soccer specialist are history.

Because soccer is an international game, the rules and regulations must be standard throughout the world. The governing body of world soccer is the Federation Internationale de Football Association (FIFA). More than 170 nations, including the United States, are members of FIFA. In 1913 the United States Soccer Football Association (USSFA) was founded and approved as a member of FIFA. Its name was later changed to the United States Soccer Federation (USSF). The various professional and amateur associations in the United States are organized under the auspices of the USSF. In 1974 the United States Youth Soccer Association (USYSA) was established as an affiliate of the USSF to administer and promote the sport for players under 19 years of age.

Playing the Game

Soccer is played on a larger field than any sport except polo (where horses do most of the work!). The field is commonly called a *pitch*. A regulation game consists of two 45-minute periods of virtually nonstop action. There are no time-outs and few substitutions. It is not surprising that soccer players are among the fittest of all athletes.

A soccer match is played between two teams of 11 players each. Each team defends a goal and tries to score in the opponent's goal. Each team designates one goalkeeper whose job is to protect the team's goal. The goalkeeper is allowed to control the ball with his or her hands within the penalty area, an area 44 yards wide and 18 yards from the endline. Field players may not use their hands or arms to control the ball, but instead they must use their feet, legs, body, or head. Goals are tallied by kicking or heading the ball into the opponent's goal. Each goal counts as one point, and the team that scores the most goals wins the match.

The alignment of the 10 field players can vary. Most systems of play deploy three or four defenders, four or five midfielders, and two or three forwards. Players are permitted to move anywhere on the playing field although each has specific responsibilities within the system of play used by the team. (See chapter 10 for more on team organization.)

A coin toss generally determines which team kicks off to start the game. Once play begins, the action is virtually continuous. The clock stops only after a goal is scored, on a penalty kick, or at the discretion of the referee. After a goal, the team scored against re-starts play with a kickoff at the center of the field.

Rules of Play

Soccer is a simple game with only 17 basic rules. The official FIFA laws of the game are standard throughout the world and pertain to all international competition. (Minor modifications of the official FIFA laws are permissible for youth and school-sponsored programs in the United States. These modifications may involve the field size, size and weight of the ball, size of the goals, allowed number of substitutes, and duration of the game.)

Playing Field

The soccer field must be 100 to 130 yards long and 50 to 100 yards wide. The length must always exceed the width. (For international matches the length must be 110 to 120 yards and the width 70 to 80 yards.)

Distinctive lines no more than 5 inches wide mark the *field area*. As shown in Diagram 1, the end boundaries of the field are called the *goal lines*, and the side boundaries are called the *touchlines*. The *halfway line* divides the playing area into two equal halves, and the *center spot* marks the center of the field. A *center circle* with a radius of 10 yards surrounds the center spot.

A *goal* is positioned at each end of the field on the center of the goal line. The dimensions of each goal are 8 feet high and 24 feet wide. The *goal area* is a rectangular box drawn along each goal line. It is formed by two lines drawn at right angles to the goal line, 6 yards from each goalpost. These lines extend 6 yards onto the field of play and are joined by a line drawn parallel with the goal line.

The *penalty area*, a rectangular box drawn along each goal line, is formed by two lines drawn at right angles to the goal line 18 yards from each goalpost. The lines extend 18 yards onto the field of play and are joined by a line drawn parallel with the goal line. The goal area is enclosed within the penalty area.

Located within the penalty area is the *penalty spot*. The penalty spot is marked 12 yards front and center of the midpoint of the goal line. Penalty kicks are taken from the penalty

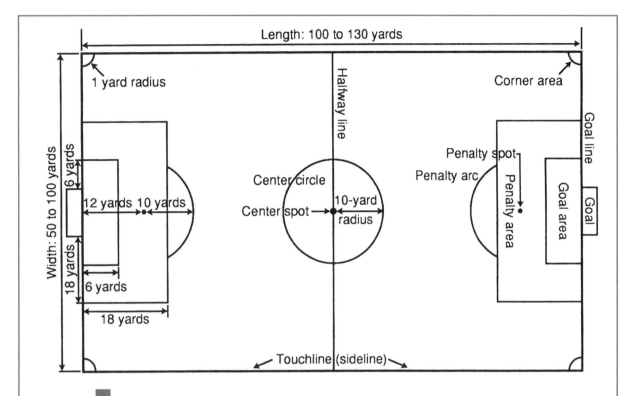

Diagram 1   Official soccer field.

spot. The *penalty arc* with a radius of 10 yards from the penalty spot is drawn outside the penalty area.

A *corner area* with a radius of 1 yard is marked at each corner of the field. Corner kicks are taken from within the corner area.

Equipment

The soccer ball is spherical and made of leather or other approved materials. The official FIFA ball is 27 to 28 inches in circumference and weighs between 14 and 16 ounces. The regulation-size adult soccer ball is designated internationally as the Size #5 ball. Smaller balls (Size #4 and Size #3) are sometimes used for youth games.

The required attire for a field player consists of a jersey or shirt, shorts, socks, shinguards, and shoes. The goalkeeper wears a shirt and shorts with padding at the elbows and hips in colors that distinguish him or her from the other players and the referee. Players are not permitted to wear any article of clothing that the referee considers a potential danger to another player. For example, watches, chains, or other forms of jewelry are usually forbidden.

Officials

An appointed referee officiates at each game. The referee enforces the laws of the game and has ultimate authority on the field. Two linesmen assist the referee. The linesmen indicate when the ball is out of play (subject to the decision of the referee) and determine which team is entitled to the throw-in, goal kick, or corner kick. They also assist the referee in determining when offside violations have occurred.

Start of Play

A player takes a placekick from the center spot of the field to initiate play. Opponents must position themselves outside the center circle in their own half of the field. The ball is "in play" when it travels into the opponent's half of the field the distance of its own circumference. The kicker is not permitted to play the ball a second time until another player touches it. A similar placekick restarts the game after a goal has been scored and also begins the second half of play. A goal cannot be scored directly from the kickoff.

Ball in and out of Play

The ball is considered "out of play" when it completely crosses a touchline or goal line, whether on the ground or in the air, or when the referee stops the game. The ball is in play at all other times, including

■ rebounds from a goalpost, crossbar, or corner flag onto the field of play;
■ rebounds off the referee or linesmen when they are in the field of play; and
■ intervals while a decision is pending on a supposed infringement of the laws.

If the referee is unsure of who last touched a ball that traveled out of the field area, play restarts with a *drop ball* at the spot where the ball was last in play. The referee drops the ball between two opposing players who cannot attempt to gain possession until the ball contacts the ground.

When the ball travels out of play over a sideline, either on the ground or in the air, it is returned into play by a *throw-in* from the spot where it left the playing field. A player from the team opposite to that of the player who last touched the ball takes the throw-in. The thrower must hold the ball with both hands and deliver it from behind and over his or her head. The player must face the field of play with each foot touching the sideline or the ground outside the sideline at the moment the ball is released. The ball is considered in play immediately after it crosses the touchline onto the field of play. The thrower may not touch the ball a second time until it has been played by another player. A throw-in is awarded to the opposing team if the ball is improperly released onto the field of play. A goal cannot be scored directly from a throw-in.

A ball last touched by a member of the attacking team that passes over the goal line, excluding the portion of the line between the goalposts and under the crossbar, is returned to play by a *goal kick* awarded to the defending team. The goal kick is taken from a spot within that half of the goal area nearest to where the ball crossed the goal line. The ball is back in play once it has traveled outside the penalty area. The kicker cannot play the ball a second time until a teammate or an opponent touches it. A goal kick cannot be played directly to the goalkeeper within the penalty area. All opposing players must position themselves outside the penalty area when a goal kick is taken. A goal cannot be scored directly off a goal kick.

A ball last touched by a member of the defending team that passes over the goal line, excluding the portion of the line between the goalposts and under the crossbar, is returned to play by a *corner kick* awarded to the attacking team. The corner kick is taken from within the quarter circle of the corner nearest the spot where the ball left the playing area. Defending players must position themselves at least 10 yards from the ball until it is played. The kicker is not permitted to play the ball a second time until another player touches it. A goal may be scored directly from a corner kick.

Scoring

A goal is scored when the ball passes completely over the goal line, between the goalposts and under the crossbar, provided it has not been thrown, carried, or intentionally propelled by an arm or hand of a player of the attacking team. Each goal counts as one point. The team scoring the most goals during a contest wins the game. The game is termed a *draw* if both teams score an equal number of goals during regulation time.

Offside

All players should be familiar with the offside law. A player is in an *offside position* if he or she is nearer the opponent's goal line than the ball is at the *moment the ball is played* unless

- the player is in his or her own half of the field or
- at least two opponents are as near their own goal line as the player is.

Just because a player is in an offside position does not mean that he or she must be declared offside. A player is declared offside and penalized for being in an offside position only if, at the moment the ball touches or is played by a teammate, the referee judges the player to be

- interfering with play or with an opponent or
- seeking to gain an advantage by being in an offside position.

A player is not offside under the following conditions:

- Merely by being in an offside position
- Receiving the ball directly from a goal kick, corner kick, or throw-in

The punishment for infringement of the offside law is an indirect free kick awarded to the opposing team at the spot where the offside occurred. It is important to consider that the referee shall judge offside at the instant the ball is played and not at the moment the player receives the ball. For example, a player who is onside at the moment the ball is played does not become offside if he or she moves forward into an offside position to receive the pass while the ball is in flight.

Free Kicks

There are two types of free kicks—direct and indirect. A goal can be scored directly by the kicker from a *direct free kick*. To score from an *indirect free kick* the ball must be played or touched by a player other than the kicker before it passes over the goal line. Defending players must position at least 10 yards from the ball for both direct and indirect free kicks. The only instance in which defending players can position closer than 10 yards to the ball is when the attacking team has been awarded an indirect free kick within 10 yards of the defending team's goal. In that situation defending players can stand on their goal line between the goalposts in an attempt to prevent the kick from entering the goal.

When a player takes a free kick from within his or her own penalty area, all opposing players must remain outside the area and position at least 10 yards from the ball. The ball must be stationary when the kick is taken and is in play once it has traveled the distance of its circumference and beyond the penalty area. The goalkeeper may not receive the ball into his or her hands and then kick it into play. If the ball is not kicked directly into play beyond the penalty area, the kick must be retaken. If the kicker touches the ball a second time before another player touches it, then the opposing team is awarded an indirect free kick.

Fouls and Misconduct

Fouls are either *direct* or *indirect*. A player who intentionally commits any of the following nine offenses will be penalized by the award of a *direct free kick* to the opposing team at the spot where the foul occurred:

- Kicking or attempting to kick an opponent
- Tripping an opponent
- Jumping at an opponent
- Charging an opponent in a violent or dangerous manner
- Charging an opponent from behind unless the opponent is obstructing the player from the ball
- Striking or attempting to strike an opponent or spitting at him or her
- Holding an opponent
- Pushing an opponent
- Carrying, striking, or propelling the ball with a hand or arm (This violation does not apply to the goalkeeper within his or her penalty area.)

If a player on the defending team intentionally commits a direct-kick offense within his or her own penalty area, he or she is penalized by the award of a *penalty kick* to the opposing team.

Indirect free kicks result from the following rule infractions:

- Playing in a manner the referee considers to be dangerous to you or another player.
- Charging an opponent with your shoulder when the ball is not within playing distance of the players involved. (Charging with the shoulder is legal if you are attempting to play the ball.)
- Intentionally obstructing an opponent when not attempting to play the ball.
- Charging the goalkeeper except when he or she has possession of the ball or has moved outside of the goal area.
- The goalkeeper takes more than four steps while in possession of the ball without releasing it into play (the so-called four-step rule).
- The goalkeeper indulges in tactics that the referee rules are designed to waste time, delay the game, and give an unfair advantage to the goalkeeper's own team.
- Violation of the goalkeeper backpass rule (see below).
- Violation of the offside rule.

Goalkeeper Backpass Rule

FIFA recently instituted a major rule change involving the goalkeeper. The *Laws of the Game* now state that the goalkeeper is not permitted to receive the ball in his or her hands after it has been deliberately kicked to him or her by a teammate. The kick must be a deliberate pass for this rule to take effect; a deflection, for example, is not penalized. Violation of the backpass rule results in the award of an indirect free kick to the opposing team at the spot of the infraction.

Players may use their head, chest, or knees to intentionally pass the ball to their goal-keeper. However, if a player uses a deliberate trick to circumvent the backpass rule (e.g., uses his or her feet to flip the ball in the air to head it to goalkeeper), the player will be guilty of "ungentlemanly behavior" and officially cautioned. The opposing team is awarded an indirect free kick from the place where the foul was committed.

Cautions and Ejections

It is the referee's discretion to reprimand a player who continually commits flagrant violations of the laws. The referee issues a *yellow card* to officially caution a player. A yellow card violation conveys a warning to the player that he or she will be ejected from the game if similar violations continue. The referee issues a *red card* to signal that a player has been ejected from the game. A player can be sent off the field and shown the red card if, in the opinion of the referee, he or she

- is guilty of violent conduct,
- is guilty of serious foul play,
- uses foul or abusive language, or
- is guilty of a second cautionable offense after already having received one caution.

The guilty player cannot return to the game and cannot be replaced by a substitute.

Penalty Kick

The most severe sanction for a direct foul, other than ejection from the game, is the penalty kick. A penalty kick results when a player commits a direct foul offense within his or her team's penalty area; it can be awarded irrespective of the position of the ball. The kick is taken from the penalty spot 12 yards front and center of the goal. All players except the kicker and the goalkeeper must position outside the penalty area at least 10 yards from the penalty spot. The goalkeeper must stand on the goal line between the goalposts and is not permitted to move his or her feet until the ball has been played. The kicker must kick the ball forward and cannot touch it a second time until it has been played by another player. The ball is in play once it has traveled the distance of its circumference. A goal can be scored directly from a penalty kick. Time should be extended at halftime or the end of regulation time to allow a penalty kick to be taken.

Warming up for Success

Prior to every practice or game you should perform a series of warm-up activities. The primary objectives of warm-up exercises are to elevate muscle temperature, promote increased blood flow to the working muscles, and stretch the major muscle groups. A warm-up improves your muscular contraction and reflex time, increases suppleness, and helps to prevent next-day soreness. A thorough warm-up also reduces the likelihood of muscle and joint injuries.

How long and hard should I warm-up? is an issue of concern to many athletes and coaches. Individual needs vary, and there is no hard and steadfast answer to that question. Environmental conditions, such as temperature and humidity, must also be taken into account. You probably will not have to warm up quite as long on a hot, humid afternoon in June as you would on a cold, blustery day in November. As a general guideline, warm up for 15 to 20 minutes at sufficient intensity to break a sweat. Sweating indicates an elevation in muscle temperature.

Begin your warm-up by increasing the blood flow to your muscles, something coaches commonly refer to as "getting your blood moving." You can accomplish this with 5 to 10 minutes of activity that elevates your heart rate from its resting state. Light dribbling with the ball or interpassing with a teammate while jogging will usually suffice. Next, perform a series of stretching exercises that work all of the major muscle groups used in soccer.

Flexibility is the range of possible movement around a joint or series of joints. Static stretching is the preferred method of increasing your range of motion. Slowly extend the target muscle or group of muscles to its greatest possible length without discomfort. A slow, steady extension of the muscle will inhibit firing of the stretch reflex, the body's built-in safeguard against overstretching. Don't bounce or jerk! Hold the stretch for 30 to 60 seconds, relax, and then move gently into a deeper stretch for 30 to 60 seconds. Stretch each muscle group twice. Be sure to address the following muscle groups:

- Hamstrings
- Quadriceps
- Back
- Groin
- Calves and Achilles tendons
- Neck

Never compete with teammates when performing flexibility exercises. Measure progress against your own standards and initial state of flexibility. Your objective is to improve your range of motion in a safe, injury-free manner, not to outstretch your friends. Conclude your warm-up with exercises designed to develop or maintain muscular strength in the following muscle groups:

- Abdominals
- Legs
- Arms and chest

At the end of each practice session or after a game, spend a few minutes allowing your heart rate and body functions to return to their resting state. During this cool-down time, perform a stretching exercise for each major muscle group. Stretching after a hard practice or a game will help to prevent next-day soreness. Remember, don't bounce or jerk when extending your muscles. Assume the stretch position, hold that position, then relax for a few seconds. Repeat each stretch twice.

International and National Associations

The following organizations are under the auspices of FIFA and administer soccer competition in the United States. The United States Soccer Federation directs amateur and professional soccer competition. The National Collegiate Athletic Association (NCAA), the National Association for Intercollegiate Athletes (NAIA), or the National Junior College Athletic Association (NJCAA) control collegiate competition for both men and women. Questions or requests for information should be directed to the appropriate organization.

International Organization

Federation Internationale de Football Association (FIFA)
FIFA House, Hitzigweg 11
8030 Zurich, Switzerland
Phone 41-1/384-9595

National Organizations

American Youth Soccer Organization (AYSO)
5403 W. 138th St.
Hawthorne, CA 90250
Phone 310-643-6455

National Soccer Coaches Association of America (NSCAA)
4220 Shawnee Mission Pkwy., Ste. 105 B
Fairway, KS 66205
Phone 800-458-0678

United States Soccer Federation (USSF)
U.S. Soccer House
1801–1811 South Prairie Ave.
Chicago, IL 60616
Phone 312-808-1300

United States Youth Soccer Association (USYSA)
Campbell Business Center
899 Presidential Drive, Ste. 117
Richardson, TX 75081
Phone 214-235-4499

Scholastic Organizations

National Association of Intercollegiate Athletics (NAIA)
6120 S. Yale Ave., Ste. 1450
Tulsa, OK 74136
Phone 918-494-8828

National Collegiate Athletic Association (NCAA)
6201 College Blvd.
Overland Park, KS 66211-2422
Phone 913-339-1906

National Junior College Athletic Association (NJCAA)
P.O. Box 7305
Colorado Springs, CO 80933-7305
Phone 719-590-9788

STEP 1

PASSING AND RECEIVING: THE ESSENCE OF TEAMWORK

Soccer is a truly team game. Although individual brilliance can be used to advantage on occasion, you will rarely if ever see a player dribble the length of the field to score a spectacular goal. In most cases a team's success depends on its players working in combination. For the team to maintain possession of the ball and create scoring opportunities, its members must develop solid passing and receiving skills. These essential skills complement one another because each passed ball should be received and controlled by a teammate. That doesn't always happen, but why not set your sights high and strive toward that goal?

Why Are Passing and Receiving Skills Important?

A soccer team consists of 10 field players and a goalkeeper. Passing and receiving skills form the vital thread that links these 11 individuals into one smoothly functioning unit that is greater than the sum of its parts. Accuracy, pacing, and the timing of release are critical ingredients for successful passing combinations. You must also be able to receive and control the ball skillfully as it arrives from a teammate. Poor passing and receiving skills will eventually result in loss of possession and wasted scoring opportunities.

Passing and Receiving Ground Balls

A rolling ball is much easier to pass and receive than one dropping from the air. With that in mind, you will benefit by passing the ball on the ground whenever possible. In the discussion that follows you'll first read about the various techniques used to pass the ball on the ground and then learn how to work on the proper ways to receive and control rolling balls.

Passing Ground Balls

There are three basic techniques for passing the ball on the ground: inside of the foot, outside of the foot, and instep. Your choice of technique depends on the situation.

Inside-of-the-Foot Pass

The most basic passing skill and the first that you should master is commonly called the *push pass* because the inside surface of the foot actually pushes the ball. The inside-of-the-foot technique is used to play the ball over distances of 5 to 15 yards. Execution is quite simple. Face the target and square your shoulders as you approach the ball. Plant your balance (nonkicking) foot beside the ball and point it toward the target. Position your kicking foot sideways

FIGURE 1.1 **KEYS TO SUCCESS**

INSIDE-OF-THE FOOT PASS

Preparation

1. Face target ___
2. Plant balance foot beside ball ___
3. Point balance foot toward target ___
4. Square shoulders and hips to target ___
5. Flex balance leg slightly at knee ___
6. Swing kicking leg backward ___
7. Position kicking foot sideways ___
8. Arms out to sides for balance ___
9. Head steady ___
10. Focus on the ball ___

Execution

1. Body over the ball ___
2. Swing kicking leg forward ___
3. Keep kicking foot firm ___
4. Contact center of ball with inside surface of foot ___

Follow-Through

1. Transfer weight forward ___
2. Generate momentum through ball ___
3. Smooth follow-through ___

and point your toes up and away from the midline of your body. Contact the center of the ball with the inside surface of your kicking foot. Make sure that your foot is firmly positioned as you follow through with the kicking motion (see Figure 1.1).

Outside-of-the-Foot Pass

At times you will have to release a pass while dribbling at speed; at other times you may want to pass the ball diagonally to the right or left. For these situations the outside-of-the-foot pass is your best choice.

This technique involves an element of deception and is less predictable to opponents than the inside-of-the-foot pass.

Use the outside-of-the foot technique for short- and medium-distance passes. Plant your balance foot slightly behind and to the side of the ball. Extend the kicking foot down and rotate it slightly inward. Use an inside-out kicking motion as you contact the inside half of the ball with the outside surface of your instep. Keep your foot firmly positioned. For passing distances of 5 to 10 yards, use a short, snaplike kick-

FIGURE
1.2

KEYS TO SUCCESS

OUTSIDE-OF-THE-FOOT PASS

Preparation

1. Plant balance foot slightly behind and to side of ball ___
2. Point balance foot forward ___
3. Flex balance leg at knee ___
4. Swing kicking leg back behind balance leg ___
5. Extend kicking foot downward and rotate inward ___
6. Arms out to sides for balance ___
7. Head steady ___
8. Focus on the ball ___

Execution

1. Head down and body over ball ___
2. Snap kicking leg forward ___
3. Keep kicking foot firmly positioned ___
4. Contact ball on outside surface of instep ___
5. Contact inside half of ball ___

Follow-Through

1. Transfer weight forward ___
2. Use an inside-out kicking motion ___
3. Complete follow-through of the kicking leg ___

ing motion of the lower leg. For longer passes use a more complete follow-through to generate greater distance and velocity (see Figure 1.2).

Instep Pass

Use the instep pass to play the ball when the distance is 25 yards or greater. The instep is the portion of your foot covered by the shoe laces. It provides a hard, flat surface with which to contact the ball. To execute the instep pass, approach the ball from a

slight angle. Plant your balance foot beside the ball with the leg slightly flexed. Square your hips and shoulders to the intended target. As you draw back the kicking leg, extend and firmly position the kicking foot. Keep your head steady and focus on the ball. Use a complete follow-through motion as you drive your instep through the point of contact with the ball. The kicking mechanics are very similar to those used when shooting (see Figure 1.3).

FIGURE
1.3 **KEYS TO SUCCESS**

INSTEP PASS

Preparation

1. Approach ball from behind at slight angle ___
2. Plant balance foot beside ball ___
3. Point balance foot toward target ___
4. Flex balance leg at knee ___
5. Square shoulders and hips to target ___
6. Draw back kicking leg ___
7. Kicking foot extended and firm ___
8. Knee of kicking leg over ball ___
9. Arms out to sides for balance ___
10. Head steady ___
11. Focus on the ball ___

Execution

1. Transfer weight forward ___
2. Powerful snaplike motion of kicking leg ___
3. Kicking foot firm ___
4. Contact the center of the ball with instep ___

Follow-Through

1. Generate momentum through the ball ___
2. Weight centered over ball of balance foot ___
3. Follow-through to chest level ___

Receiving Ground Balls

Again, depending on the situation, you have the option of using either the inside of the foot or the outside of the foot to receive and control ground passes. In either case you must make your body a "soft target" by withdrawing the receiving surface as the ball arrives to cushion the impact.

Inside-of-the-Foot Reception

You can receive and control a ball with the inside surface of your foot when you are not under immediate pressure from an opponent. Align yourself with the oncoming ball and move forward to receive it. Extend your receiving leg and foot to meet the ball as it arrives. Firmly position the receiving foot sideways with toes pointed up and away from the midline of

FIGURE 1.4

FIGURE 1.4 **KEYS TO SUCCESS**

INSIDE-OF-THE-FOOT RECEPTION

Preparation

1. Square shoulders and hips with oncoming ball ___
2. Move toward ball ___
3. Extend receiving leg to meet ball ___
4. Position receiving foot sideways ___
5. Keep receiving foot firm ___
6. Head steady and watch the ball ___

Execution

1. Receive ball on inside surface of foot ___
2. Withdraw foot to cushion impact ___
3. Control ball into the space away from nearby opponent ___

Follow-Through

1. Head up and watch the field ___
2. Push ball in direction of next movement ___

the body. Withdraw your foot as the ball arrives to cushion its impact. Don't stop (trap) the ball completely. Rather, receive and control the ball in the direction of your next movement or into the space away from a nearby opponent (see Figure 1.4).

Outside-of-the-Foot Reception

There are times when you must receive a pass while tightly marked by an opponent. In this situation the inside-of-the-foot technique is not always appropri-

ate because the defending player may be able to reach in with his or her foot to kick the ball free. Use your body to protect the ball from a challenging opponent by receiving it with the outside surface of your foot. Position sideways as the ball arrives with your body between the opponent and the ball. Receive the ball with the foot farthest from the opponent. Rotate your receiving foot inward and downward and receive the ball on the outside surface of your instep (see Figure 1.5).

FIGURE 1.5 **KEYS TO SUCCESS**

OUTSIDE-OF-THE-FOOT RECEPTION

Preparation

1. Position sideways between ball and opponent ___
2. Knees flexed with low center of gravity ___
3. Prepare to control ball with foot farthest from opponent ___
4. Extend receiving foot down and rotate inward ___
5. Keep receiving foot firm ___
6. Head steady and watch the ball ___

Execution

1. Receive ball on outside surface of instep ___
2. Withdraw receiving leg and foot upon impact ___
3. Turn ball into space away from nearby opponent ___
4. Readjust body position to shield ball from opponent ___

Follow-Through

1. Head up and watch the field ___
2. Push ball in direction of next movement ___

GROUND BALL SUCCESS STOPPERS

It may appear relatively easy to pass and receive a rolling ball. The task is not so simple, however, if an opponent is trying his or her hardest to steal the ball from you! Most passing and receiving errors are due to improper technique, lack of concentration, or failure to choose the most appropriate option for a particular situation. Although we would all like to be perfect soccer players, don't be too hard on yourself. Expect mistakes to occur until you become comfortable executing the skills and get the opportunity to practice them under game-simulated conditions. Here is a list of common errors players make when passing and receiving ground balls and suggestions for correcting those errors.

Error	Correction
Inside-of-the-Foot Pass	
1. Ball leaves the ground.	1. Contacting the ball too far forward on your foot, near the toes, or too far underneath the ball will cause it to pop upward into the air. Contact the center of the ball with the inside surface of your kicking foot between the ankle and toes.
2. Poor accuracy.	2. Plant your balance foot beside the ball and pointed toward the target. Square hips and shoulders. Keep your head steady as you contact the ball.
3. Pass lacks velocity or pace.	3. Keep kicking foot firm. Transfer your weight forward as the kicking foot contacts the ball. Use a smooth follow-through motion.
4. You approach the ball from a severe angle and attempt to kick across your body.	4. Approach from directly behind the ball. Square shoulders and hips to target as your foot contacts the ball. Pass in the direction you are facing.
Outside-of-the-Foot Pass	
1. Ball leaves the ground.	1. Plant your balance foot slightly behind and to the side of the ball. Your kicking foot should be pointed down and rotated inward with your knee over the ball at the moment of contact. Do not lean back. Keep your head steady and focus on the ball.
2. Pass lacks pace.	2. Keep the kicking foot firm and use a short, powerful snaplike motion of the kicking leg. Contact the ball with as much foot surface area as possible. For longer passes use a complete follow-through motion of the kicking leg.
3. Too much spin to the ball.	3. Contact the ball just left or right of its vertical midline, not along its outer edge.

Error	Correction
Instep Pass	
1. Pass travels upward.	1. Usually occurs when you plant your balance foot too far behind the ball and lean back as you kick it. Plant your balance foot beside the ball. This will enable you to position the knee of your kicking leg over the ball and fully extend the kicking foot as you contact the ball.
2. Poor accuracy.	2. Square your shoulders and hips with the target as you prepare to kick the ball. Keep your kicking foot firm as it contacts the center of the ball.
3. Too much spin on the ball and it swerves away from the target.	3. Strike the ball directly through its center with the large flat surface of the instep.
Receiving With Inside of the Foot	
1. The ball rolls over your foot and out of your range of control.	1. You probably tried to receive the ball too far forward on your foot. Contact the center of the ball with the inside surface of your foot midway between the toes and heel.
2. The ball rebounds off your foot.	2. Always provide a soft target. Withdraw the receiving surface as the ball arrives to cushion its impact.
3. The ball rolls under your foot.	3. You positioned your receiving foot too high off the ground and probably took your eye off the ball as well. Keep your head steady and focus on the ball. Raise your receiving foot about 1 inch off the ground and contact the center of the ball with the inside surface of your foot.
Receiving With Outside of the Foot	
1. The ball bounces away from you.	1. Withdraw your receiving foot as the ball arrives to cushion its impact.
2. An opponent reaches in with his or her foot and kicks the ball away from you.	2. Protect the ball at all times. Position your body sideways and receive the ball with the foot farthest from the opponent. Readjust your position in response to your opponent's movement.
3. The defender cuts in front of you and intercepts the pass.	3. Always move toward the ball as you prepare to receive it. You must be the first player to the ball.

Passing Lofted Balls

Although in most situations you should pass the ball on the ground, there are times when a lofted pass is your best choice. For example, a defending player may be blocking the passing lane between you and a teammate who is moving into a dangerous attacking position. Or you may decide to chip a ball into the open space behind the opposing defense for a teammate to run on to. You can even use a lofted pass to score a goal when the opposing goalkeeper drifts too far forward from his or her goal line. To take advantage of these special situations, you must become adept at accurately chipping the ball. Players use two basic techniques, the *short chip* and the *long chip*, to pass the ball through the air. Your choice of technique depends on the distance the ball must travel.

Short-Chip Pass

Use this technique to play the ball to a teammate over an opponent(s) who is blocking the passing lane. This situation may occur during the normal course of play or when opponents have formed a wall of players to defend against a free kick. A properly executed chip pass enables you to exploit the open space behind defending players.

Approach from behind the ball at a slight angle. Plant your balance foot beside the ball and draw back your kicking leg with foot extended. Square your shoulders with the target. Keep your kicking foot extended and firmly positioned as you drive (wedge) it beneath the ball. Use a short, powerful snaplike kicking motion with minimal follow-through. Wedging your foot underneath the ball will impart slight backspin on the pass, which makes a "softer" pass (see Figure 1.6).

FIGURE
1.6   **KEYS TO SUCCESS**

SHORT-CHIP PASS

Preparation

1. Approach ball from a slight angle ___
2. Plant balance foot beside the ball ___
3. Flex balance leg ___
4. Draw back kicking leg ___
5. Extend kicking foot ___
6. Arms out to sides for balance ___
7. Head steady ___
8. Focus on the ball ___

Execution

1. Place knee of kicking leg over ball ___
2. Lean slightly forward ___
3. Square shoulders with target ___
4. Drive instep under ball ___
5. Keep kicking foot firm ___
6. Use short, powerful kicking motion ___
7. Arms swing forward ___
8. Impart slight backspin on ball ___

Follow-Through

1. Weight moves forward over ball of balance foot ___
2. Kicking leg snaps straight ___
3. Minimal follow-through ___

Long-Chip Pass

The kicking mechanics are similar in some respects to those used for the short-chip pass. Approach from behind the ball at a slight angle. Plant your balance foot to the side and behind the ball. Note that the position of your balance foot differs slightly from the one you used for the short-chip pass. Planting your foot behind the ball allows greater follow-through motion of your kicking leg and enables you to drive the ball over longer distances. Extend your kicking foot, keep it firm, and drive your instep through the lower third of the ball. Lean back as you contact the ball (see Figure 1.7).

FIGURE 1.7

KEYS TO SUCCESS

LONG-CHIP PASS

Preparation

1. Approach the ball from a slight angle ___
2. Plant balance foot to the side and slightly behind ball ___
3. Flex the balance leg ___
4. Draw back kicking leg ___
5. Extend kicking foot ___
6. Arms out to sides for balance ___
7. Head steady ___
8. Focus on the ball ___

Execution

1. Place knee of kicking leg slightly behind ball ___
2. Lean backward slightly ___
3. Square shoulders with target ___
4. Drive instep of kicking foot through lower third of ball ___
5. Keep kicking foot firm ___
6. Arms move forward ___
7. Impart slight backspin on ball ___

Follow-Through

1. Kicking leg snaps straight ___
2. Weight moves forward over ball of the balance foot ___
3. Complete follow-through ___
4. Kicking foot to waist level or higher ___

Receiving Lofted Balls

You must also be able to receive and control balls dropping from the air. Four body surfaces—the instep, thigh, chest, and head—are commonly used to receive lofted balls. Your choice of surface depends upon the flight trajectory of the ball and whether or not you are being pressured by an opponent.

Instep

The instep provides an excellent surface with which to receive and control a ball dropping from above.

Use this technique when you are not under immediate pressure from an opponent.

Imagine that your shoe is a baseball glove and that you are going to catch the ball on the instep of your foot. The first thing that you must do is get in the proper position. Anticipate where the ball will drop and move to that spot. Face the ball and raise your receiving foot 12 to 18 inches off the ground. Extend your receiving foot parallel to the ground and keep it firmly positioned. As the ball contacts the instep, withdraw your foot downward to the ground. This movement will cushion the impact and drop the ball at your feet (see Figure 1.8).

FIGURE
1.8

KEYS TO SUCCESS

RECEIVING LOFTED BALL WITH INSTEP

Preparation

1. Move to receiving position ___
2. Square shoulders with flight of ball ___
3. Raise receiving foot 12 to 18 inches off ground ___
4. Extend receiving foot parallel to ground ___
5. Keep receiving foot firm ___
6. Flex balance leg ___
7. Arms to sides for balance ___
8. Head steady and watch the ball ___

Execution

1. Receive ball on instep ___
2. Withdraw receiving foot to ground ___
3. Drop ball within range of control ___
4. Protect ball from nearby opponents ___

Follow-Through

1. Push ball into open space ___
2. Head up and watch the field ___

Thigh

The instep is not always your best choice for receiving a lofted ball. For example, the angle at which the ball is dropping or the presence of nearby opponents sometimes makes it impossible to use the instep technique. The midthigh area is an alternative body surface that can be used to receive and control a ball dropping from above.

Anticipate the flight of the ball and move into position to receive it. If tightly marked, position your body between the opponent and the ball. Raise your receiving leg so that your thigh is parallel to the ground. Flex your balance leg slightly with arms out to the sides for balance. Receive the ball on the midthigh area and withdraw your leg downward at the instant the ball arrives. The ball should drop softly to the ground at your feet (see Figure 1.9).

FIGURE 1.9

RECEIVING LOFTED BALL WITH THIGH

  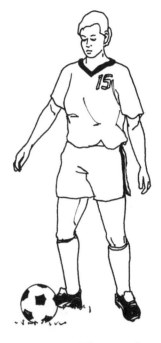

Preparation	Execution	Follow-Through
1. Position under descending ball ___	1. Receive ball on midthigh ___	1. Push ball to open space ___
2. Raise receiving leg ___	2. Withdraw thigh downward ___	2. Head up and watch the field ___
3. Thigh parallel to ground ___	3. Collect ball at feet ___	
4. Flex balance leg ___	4. Shield ball from opponent ___	
5. Arms out to sides for balance ___		
6. Head steady and watch the ball ___		

Chest

The upper central area of your chest also provides an excellent receiving surface, particularly when you are pressured by an opponent. Position yourself between the opponent and the oncoming ball. Arch your upper body slightly backward from the vertical and receive the ball on the central area of your chest. Withdraw your upper body as the ball arrives to cush-ion its impact. Attempt to control the ball into the space away from the opponent by turning your upper body in the direction you wish to move just prior to the ball contacting your chest. Although women are usually permitted to cross their arms against the chest and receive the ball on the arms, most high school and college women use the same receiving technique as men (see Figure 1.10).

FIGURE 1.10

KEYS TO SUCCESS

RECEIVING LOFTED BALL WITH CHEST

Preparation

1. Position between defender and ball ___
2. Align body with oncoming ball ___
3. Arch upper body backward ___
4. Bend knees slightly ___
5. Arms out to sides for balance ___
6. Head steady and watch the ball ___

Execution

1. Receive ball on upper chest area ___
2. Withdraw chest to cushion impact ___
3. Turn upper body as ball arrives ___
4. Control ball into space away from opponent ___

Follow-Through

1. Shield ball from opponent ___
2. Push ball in direction of next movement ___
3. Head up and watch the field ___

Head

Most of the time you use your head to pass the ball to a teammate, shoot on goal, or clear a crossed ball from the area front and center of your goal. In certain situations you can also use your head to receive and control a ball dropping from above. Successful execution of this skill requires proper technique as well as precise timing of the jump.

Move to a position beneath the descending ball. Use a two-footed takeoff to jump. Leave the ground early so as to contact the ball at the highest point of your jump. Angle your head back, focus on the ball, and receive the ball on the flat surface of your forehead. If you've properly timed your jump, you will start descending to the ground at the instant the ball contacts your forehead. The downward motion of your body will soften the impact of the ball. It should bounce a few inches upward off your forehead and then drop to your feet (see Figure 1.11).

FIGURE 1.11

KEYS TO SUCCESS

RECEIVING LOFTED BALL WITH HEAD

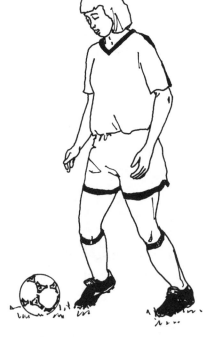

Preparation

1. Position under descending ball ___
2. Flex knees in preparation to jump ___
3. Arms extended back and to sides ___
4. Focus on the ball ___

Execution

1. Jump early ___
2. Use two-footed takeoff ___
3. Arch upper body slightly backward ___
4. Keep eyes open ___
5. Angle forehead back ___
6. Meet ball at highest point of jump ___
7. Contact ball on forehead ___
8. Withdraw head slightly upon contact ___

Follow-Through

1. Land on both feet ___
2. Drop ball to ground within range of control ___
3. Push ball into open space ___
4. Head up and watch the field ___

LOFTED BALLS SUCCESS STOPPERS

Nearly all of the beginners at my soccer camps find it difficult to pass and receive lofted balls. Don't get discouraged! It takes time to master these skills. Successful execution requires confidence, proper technique, and a great deal of practice.

Most errors that occur when passing and receiving lofted balls can be attributed to improper position of either the kicking or the receiving foot, poor balance, or both. For example, beginners may hesitate to wedge the foot underneath the ball when attempting a chip pass for fear of injury. The following review of performance errors that occur when passing and receiving lofted balls suggests how to correct them.

Error	Correction
Short-Chip Pass	
1. Trajectory of your pass is too low.	1. Contact the bottom third of the ball with the instep. Use a short, powerful kicking motion to drive your foot underneath the ball and send it over an opponent.
2. Poor accuracy.	2. Square your shoulders and hips with the target as you kick the ball. Contact the ball with as much of your instep as possible. Be sure to keep the kicking foot firm as you wedge it underneath the ball.
Long-Chip Pass	
1. The ball fails to clear defending players.	1. Plant your balance foot to the side and slightly behind the ball. Lean back as you drive the instep of your kicking foot beneath the ball.
2. Your pass is too short.	2. Extend and firmly position your kicking foot. Use a complete follow-through motion of the kicking leg.
3. Poor accuracy.	3. Square your shoulders and hips with the intended target. Contact the central, lower third of the ball with your instep. Keep your kicking foot firm as it contacts the ball.
Receiving With Your Instep	
1. The ball bounces up and out of control upon contact with your instep.	1. Preparation is everything. Raise your receiving foot to meet the ball prior to its arrival. Withdraw your foot downward at the instant the ball contacts your instep. This motion will provide a soft target to cushion the impact of the ball.
2. The ball spins back into your body after contacting your foot.	2. This occurs because your receiving foot is angled upward rather than being fully extended. Extend your receiving foot so it is approximately parallel to the ground. Receive the ball on the full instep.

Error	Correction
Receiving With Your Thigh	
1. The ball bounces up and out of control upon contact with your thigh.	1. This occurs because your leg is moving upward as the ball arrives. Raise your thigh into the proper receiving position prior to the arrival of the ball. Withdraw your leg downward as the ball contacts your thigh.
2. The ball bounces forward off your thigh and out of your range of control.	2. This usually occurs when you have received the ball too far forward on your thigh (near the knee cap) or because your leg was positioned incorrectly. Position your thigh parallel to the ground as the ball arrives. Receive the ball on midthigh, approximately halfway between your knee and hip. This area of your leg provides a large, soft receiving surface.
Receiving With Your Chest	
1. The ball rebounds off your chest and out of your range of control.	1. Receive the ball just right or left of center chest where the muscle and soft tissue provide an excellent receiving surface. Withdraw your upper body (chest) backward a few inches as the ball makes contact.
2. The ball skips off your chest, over your shoulder, and past you.	2. This occurs because you have arched your upper body too far back. Arch backward only a few inches from the vertical position as you receive the ball.
Receiving With Your Head	
1. The ball bounces off your forehead and out of your range of control.	1. You jumped too late and as a result were still moving upward as the ball contacted your forehead. Correct timing of the jump is critical to success. You must leave the ground early so that your body is just beginning to descend as the ball arrives. Withdraw your head slightly as the ball makes contact to provide a softer receiving surface.
2. The ball glances sideways off your head.	2. Receive the ball on the large, flat surface of the forehead just above your eyebrows. Keep your neck firm, head steady, and focus on the ball at all times.

PASSING AND RECEIVING

DRILLS

1. "Pingers" off the Wall

Position yourself with a ball approximately 5 yards from a wall or kickboard. Use the inside-of-the-foot technique to "ping" the ball off the wall so it rebounds back to you. Receive and control each rebound with either the inside or the outside of the foot; then immediately pass it off the wall again. This is commonly referred to as two-touch passing—control the ball with your first touch and pass it with the second touch. Alternate passing with right and left feet.

Success Goal = 35 of 40 two-touch passes off the wall without error ___

Success Check
- Balance foot pointing toward target ___
- Passing foot firmly positioned ___
- Contact center of ball ___

To Increase Difficulty
- Move 10 yards from wall.
- Increase speed of repetition.
- Make all passes with your weaker foot.

To Decrease Difficulty
- Move closer to wall.
- Allow three touches to receive and pass the ball.
- Make all passes with your stronger foot.

2. "Rapid Fire" Partner Pass

Stand facing a partner 8 yards away. Position two cones to represent a goal 2 yards wide midway between you and your teammate. Attempt to pass a ball back and forth as rapidly as possible through the cones using the inside-of-the-foot technique. Control each pass with the inside or outside surface of your foot. Alternate passing with left and right feet and use two-touch passes only. Award one team point for each ball passed between the cones using only two touches. Play for 60 seconds. Compare your point total against other pairs of teammates. Repeat for 10 rounds.

Success Goal = Score the most points ___

Success Check
- Passing foot firm ___
- First touch to prepare ball, second touch to pass ___
- Contact center of ball ___

To Increase Difficulty
- Increase passing distance to 12 yards.
- Increase time to 90 seconds per round.
- Reduce goal width to 1 yard.

To Decrease Difficulty
- Decrease passing distance to 5 yards.
- Allow three touches to receive and pass the ball.
- Increase goal width to 3 yards.

3. Chip to Chest

Face a teammate at a distance of 5 yards. Use a short, powerful kicking motion to chip a stationary ball to your partner's chest. He or she receives the ball on the chest and then returns the ball to you with an inside-of-the-foot pass. Execute 25 chip passes with each foot, then change roles with your partner.

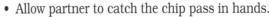

Success Goal =

40 of 50 passes chipped to partner's chest ___

40 of 50 balls controlled with chest and dropped to feet within range of control ___

To Increase Difficulty

- Decrease chip pass distance to 3 yards to steepen the required trajectory of pass.
- Chip a rolling ball to partner's chest.

To Decrease Difficulty

- Allow partner to catch the chip pass in hands.

Success Check

- Balance foot beside ball ___
- Square shoulders and hips to target ___
- Drive instep underneath ball ___
- Minimal follow-through ___

4. Long-Distance Pass

Position yourself 25 to 30 yards from a teammate. Use either the instep or outside-of-the-foot technique to pass a ball back and forth along the ground to your partner. Use only two touches to receive and pass the ball and alternate passes with left and right feet. Receive the ball with either the inside or outside of the foot. Perform 20 passes with each foot. The player receiving the pass should not have to move more than 2 yards in any direction to collect the ball.

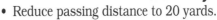

Success Goal =

32 of 40 passes accurately passed within 2 yards of your partner ___

35 of 40 balls received and returned to partner using only two touches ___

To Increase Difficulty

- Chip the ball to partner.
- Increase passing distance.
- Pass with weaker foot only.

To Decrease Difficulty

- Reduce passing distance to 20 yards.
- Allow three-touch passing.
- Pass with stronger foot only.

Success Check

- Move toward ball to receive it ___
- Provide a soft receiving surface ___
- Prepare ball with first touch ___

5. Pass and Support

Perform this drill with several teammates. Divide yourselves into two equal-size groups. Groups line up in single file facing each other at a distance of 12 to 15 yards. The first player in Group 1 passes the ball to the first player in Group 2 and then supports his or her pass by running to the end of Line 2. Use either the inside- or outside-of-the-foot technique to pass the ball. The first player in Line 2 receives the ball using the inside or outside surface of the foot, then passes it to the next player in Line 1 and immediately sprints to the end of that line. Use only two touches to receive and pass the ball. Continue the drill until each player has passed and received 30 balls.

Success Goal =

26 out of 30 passes accurately played to teammate in the opposite line ___
26 out of 30 balls controlled and passed using
only two touches ___

Success Check

• Provide a soft target ___
• Prepare ball with first touch, pass with second
touch ___
• Keep passing foot firm ___

To Increase Difficulty

• Increase passing distance to 20 yards.
• Pass with instep technique only.
• Pass with weaker foot only.
• Increase speed of repetition.
• Chip all passes through the air.

To Decrease Difficulty

• Reduce passing distance to 10 yards.
• Allow three touches to control and pass ball.

6. Over and Under

Position with a ball 10 yards front and center of a regulation goal. Remove the goal net so that a ball can be passed back and forth through the goal. A teammate faces you an equal distance from the goal on the opposite side. Pass a rolling ball through the goal to your teammate who attempts to return the ball by chipping it over the 8-foot-high crossbar. You receive and control the chip pass out of the air, then repeat the exercise. Award your partner one point for each ball chipped over the goal so that you can receive it out of the air. Award yourself one point for each ball received and dropped to the ground within your range of control. Receive 40 chip passes from your partner, then switch roles and chip 40 passes over the goal to your partner.

Success Goal =

30 of 40 possible points passing ___
30 of 40 possible points receiving ___

Success Check

Passing:
• Square shoulders and hips to target ___
• Drive instep underneath ball ___
• Short, powerful leg snap ___

Receiving:
• Select receiving surface early ___
• Withdraw receiving surface upon contact with
ball ___

To Increase Difficulty

• Chip ball with weakest foot.
• Receive the ball with a specific body surface.

To Decrease Difficulty

• Chip pass a stationary ball.
• Reduce height of the goal to 6 feet.

7. Chip and Receive in Threes

Stand opposite a teammate positioned 25 yards away. A third player (server) positions with a ball midway between you. The player in the center passes a rolling ball to you. Attempt to chip the rolling ball over the server's head to your teammate. Players rotate positions after each pass: The server moves to your original position, the player who received your chip pass moves to the middle, and you follow your pass as you move to the opposite end of the line. Continue the drill until each player has chipped and received 40 lofted balls; rotate positions after each pass. You are permitted to chip the ball with your favorite (stronger) foot.

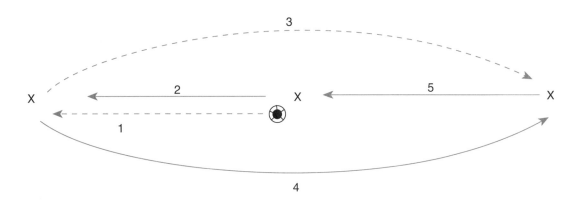

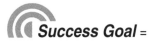 **Success Goal =**

30 of 40 passes chipped over center player that drop to the ground within 5 feet of the teammate positioned 25 yards away ___

30 of 40 lofted balls received out of the air and controlled using only two touches ___

 Success Check

Passing:
- Square shoulders and hips to target ___
- Lean back slightly ___
- Drive instep beneath ball ___
- Use sufficient follow-through ___

Receiving:
- Align body with oncoming ball ___
- Select receiving surface early ___
- Withdraw receiving surface upon contact with ball ___
- Drop ball to ground within range of control ___

To Increase Difficulty
- Increase passing distance.
- Pass with your weaker foot.
- Receive to control the ball with a specific body surface.

To Decrease Difficulty
- Reduce passing distance.
- Chip a stationary ball.

8. Passing to Moving Targets

Play with two teammates in an area approximately 35 yards square. You begin with the ball. On command, your teammates begin jogging randomly within the playing area. Pass the ball to either of your teammates using the instep or outside-of-the-foot technique. Immediately sprint to a position near the player to whom you passed the ball, receive a short return pass, turn, and pass the ball to the third player as he or she moves within the area. All passes should be 20 yards or longer, and all players, with or without the ball, should move constantly throughout the exercise. Try to use only two touches to receive and pass the ball. Execute 25 passes, then switch roles with one of your teammates. Repeat until each player has made 25 passes.

Success Goal = 20 of 25 accurate passes using only two touches ___

Success Check
- Prepare the ball with your first touch ___
- Keep passing foot firm ___
- Pass the ball so teammate can receive it without breaking stride ___

To Increase Difficulty
- Increase the passing distance.
- Kick all passes with weakest foot only.
- Chip and receive all passes out of the air.

To Decrease Difficulty
- Reduce the passing distance.
- Allow three or more touches to receive and pass the ball.
- Perform drill at half speed.

9. Soccer Dodge Ball

Play with two teams of five to seven players. Mark a playing area of approximately 30 yards square. Your team positions outside the area, each player with a ball, while the opponents station within the area without balls. On command, players from your team dribble into the area and attempt to pass to hit opponents below the knees with a ball. Opponents use quick changes of speed and direction to avoid being hit. Use the inside-of-the-foot technique for all passes. A player is awarded one point for each opponent he or she contacts below the knees with a passed ball. Play for 5 minutes, then teams switch roles and repeat. The team with the most points wins the game.

Success Goal = Pass to hit as many opponents as possible in 5 minutes ___

Success Check
- Dribble close to target ___
- Passing foot firm ___
- Contact center of ball ___

To Increase Difficulty
- Enlarge the playing area.
- Players pass with their weakest foot only.

To Decrease Difficulty
- Reduce size of playing area.

10. Numbers Passing Game

Play with five to seven teammates within a 40-yard-square area. Assign each player a number, beginning with one and continuing up through the number of players in the group. Two players each have possession of a ball to begin. On command, everyone begins to jog randomly within the area; those with a ball dribble. Dribblers locate the teammate numbered directly above them and pass to him or her. (The player with the highest number passes to Player 1 to complete the circuit.) Once play begins, all players must move continuously as they pass to the teammate numbered above them and receive passes from the teammate numbered below them. Use any of the ground pass techniques discussed in Step 1. Play nonstop for 10 minutes.

Success Goal = 5 or fewer passing errors, receiving errors, or both in a 10-minute game ___

Success Check
- Accuracy and correct pace of passes ___
- Receive ball within range of control ___
- Control the ball into the space away from imaginary defender ___

To Increase Difficulty
- Players pass the ball with their weaker foot only.
- Passes must be 25 yards or longer.
- Chip passes only.
- Add one defender to the game who tries to intercept all passes.

To Decrease Difficulty
- Reduce passing distance to 10 yards or less.
- Perform drill at half speed.

11. Possession Game

Play with three teammates. Use cones or flags to mark off a grid area approximately 12 yards square. You and two teammates form an attacking team and try to keep the ball away from the fourth player (defender) within the grid. Use any passing and receiving technique appropriate for the situation. The attacking team scores one point each time it makes eight consecutive passes without loss of possession to the defender. The passing sequence is broken if the defender steals the ball. He or she then returns the ball to the attacking team and play restarts. Attacking players are allowed a maximum of three touches to receive and pass the ball. Play for 5 minutes, then designate a new defender and repeat the game. Each player should take a turn as the defender. This exercise incorporates the game-related pressures of limited space, player movement, and an opponent challenging the ball.

Success Goal = Score a minimum of 5 points in a 5-minute game ___

Success Check
- Ground passes only ___
- Control ball into space away from defender ___
- Passing foot firm ___

To Increase Difficulty
(for Attackers)
- Reduce size of playing area.
- Impose two-touch limit to receive and pass the ball.
- Award one point for 10 consecutive passes.

To Decrease Difficulty
(for Attackers)
- Enlarge the playing area.
- Allow attackers unlimited touches to pass and receive the ball.
- Add a fourth attacker.
- Award one point for five consecutive passes.

12. Pass and Receive to Score

Play with two teams of three to five players. Outline an area of approximately 40 yards square. Use cones or flags to represent six small goals, each 2 yards wide, randomly positioned within the area. Your team begins with the ball. Each team can score in all six goals and must defend all six goals. To score, a player must complete a pass through a goal to a teammate positioned on the other side. Each goal earns one point. You may pass the ball through either side of a goal, but not twice consecutively through the same goal. Regular soccer rules apply except that teams do not change possession of the ball after a goal. Play nonstop for 15 minutes and keep track of points. Use any of the passing and receiving skills discussed in Step 1.

Success Goal = Score more team points than opponents ___

Success Check
• Accuracy and correct pace of passes ___
• Receive and control each pass into space away from opponent ___
• Change the point of attack frequently ___

To Increase Difficulty
• Decrease the size of the playing area.
• Decrease goal size to 1 yard.
• Designate two neutral players who always play with the defending team, giving the defenders a two-player advantage over the attackers.

To Decrease Difficulty
• Make the goals larger.
• Increase the number of goals.
• Designate two neutral players who always play with the team in possession, giving the attackers a two-player advantage over the defenders.

13. Toss, Receive, and Catch

Divide into two teams of three or four players. Use markers to outline a playing field of approximately 30 by 40 yards. Your team begins with the ball and tries to play "keepaway" from the opponents. Passing is accomplished by throwing rather than kicking. Players must receive each pass out of the air with their instep, thigh, chest, or head and then catch the ball in their hands before it drops to the ground. You may take up to five steps while in possession of the ball before passing to a teammate. Opponents gain possession when they intercept a pass or when you or one of your teammates fails to control the ball before it drops to the ground. Defending players may not wrestle the ball from opponents. Award one team point for 10 consecutive passes without loss of possession. Play for 20 minutes. The team scoring the most points wins the game.

Success Goal = Score more points than opponents ___

Success Check
• Align body with oncoming ball ___
• Select receiving surface early ___
• Provide a soft target ___

To Increase Difficulty
• Passes must be 10 yards or longer.
• Players must receive the ball with a specific body part (e.g., thigh only).

To Decrease Difficulty
• Add three neutral players to the game who always play with the attacking team.

14. Two-Player Team Volleyball

Play on a volleyball court with three teammates. Divide into teams of two and position on opposite side of the net. Flip a coin to determine which team gets to serve first. To serve, you must chip a stationary ball over the net from behind the endline. The receiving team can control the ball directly out of the air or after it bounces once. (This applies to all plays, not only service returns.) If the ball bounces two or more times in the opponent's court or if the receiving team fails to return the serve over the net, the serving team wins one point and retains service. A player receiving the ball is allowed three touches to control it and play it over the net or to a teammate who then plays it over the net. Once the ball has been received, however, it must be returned over the net before it drops to the ground.

A fault occurs when

- the serve or return fails to clear the net;
- the serve or return lands out of bounds;
- a ball is allowed to bounce more than once; or
- a player uses his or her arms or hands to pass or control the ball.

If the serving team commits a fault, they lose serve. If the receiving team commits a fault, the serving team gets one point. The first team to 15 points wins the game. Play the best of five games.

Success Goal = Score 15 points before opponents ___

✔ Success Check
- Position under descending ball ___
- Prepare receiving surface early ___
- Cushion impact of ball ___

To Increase Difficulty
- Require server to chip a rolling ball.
- Raise height of the net.
- Play the ball directly out of the air.
- Limit players to two touches to receive and return the ball.

To Decrease Difficulty
- Lower the net.
- Increase number of players per team.
- Serve by volleying ball out of hands.
- Allow ball to bounce twice before returning over net.

SUCCESS SUMMARY

Eleven individuals blending their talents and abilities into one close-knit, cohesive unit is the ultimate goal of every soccer team. Achieving that goal is only a pipedream, however, unless each team member possesses solid passing and receiving skills. Beginners should start by practicing passing and receiving skills in a relatively pressure-free setting. Focus on correct skill execution without having to worry about opponents trying to steal the ball from you. Progress to more game-simulated practice situations as your skill level improves and you become more confident. Add the elements of restricted space and challenging opponents. Eventually you will be able to execute the basic passing and receiving skills in a real game.

STEP 2

DRIBBLING, SHIELDING, AND TACKLING: INDIVIDUAL BALL POSSESSION

Mention the word *dribble* in a crowd of soccer enthusiasts and most assuredly you will hear someone say, Don't dribble, don't be a ball hog! Granted, excessive dribbling at inopportune times can destroy the teamwork needed to create goal-scoring opportunities. On the other hand, creative dribbling skills used in the right situations can wreak havoc on an opposing defense.

Dribbling in soccer serves the same function as dribbling in basketball—it enables you to maintain possession of the ball when you run past opponents or advance into open space. You can use various surfaces of your foot (inside, outside, instep, sole) to control the ball while dribbling. In a sense dribbling can be considered an art rather than a skill. You can develop your own style, paint your own picture so to speak, as long as it achieves the primary objective of beating an opponent while maintaining possession of the ball.

Keep in mind, however, that excessive dribbling serves no useful purpose. Refrain from dribbling to take on (beat) opponents in the defending third of the field nearest your own goal. Loss of ball possession there can easily result in an opponent's score. However, you can use dribbling skills to your advantage in the attacking third of the field near the opponent's goal. If you take on and beat an opponent in that area you've probably created a scoring opportunity for your team. Two dribbling techniques—dribbling for close control when in a confined space and dribbling for speed when advancing into open space—are important in game situations.

Shielding skills are often used in conjunction with dribbling skills to protect the ball from opponents trying to gain possession. Shield the ball by positioning your body between the ball and the opponent trying to steal it. This technique is also referred to as "screening" the ball.

The term *tackle* has a different meaning in soccer than it has in American football. In soccer you tackle the ball, not the opposing player. Three techniques—the *block tackle, poke tackle,* and *slide tackle*—are used depending on the situation. The block tackle has several advantages over the poke and slide tackle. It allows for greater body control and also puts you in a position to counterattack quickly once you gain possession of the ball. In addition, if you mistime the tackle and fail to win the ball, you are still in position to recover quickly and chase your opponent.

Why Are Dribbling, Shielding, and Tackling Skills Important?

The soccer ball is a very precious commodity—without it your team can't score goals. The fact remains, however, that there is only one ball and it must be shared by 22 players. Be assured that when you possess the ball, opponents will be trying their hardest to steal it.

Successful attacking play in part depends on each player's ability to maintain possession of the ball. The ability to beat opponents on the dribble in one-on-one situations, particularly in the attacking third of the field, and the ability to withstand the challenge of opponents trying to gain possession of the ball are critical to individual as well as team success. On the flip side of the coin, when your team is defending, you must do your part to win the ball back. Tackling is strictly a defensive skill used to strip, or steal, the ball from an opponent. All field players should be able to execute tackling skills successfully because everyone must assume defensive responsibilities when the opponents have the ball.

How to Execute Dribbling and Shielding Skills

All successful dribbling styles contain several common elements. These include sudden changes of speed and direction, body feints, deceptive foot movements, and close control of the ball. Whatever your style, be sure to include these elements in your technique.

Dribble for Close Control

You must keep close control of the ball in situations where opposing players crowd your space. Imagine that the ball is tied to your toes by a short string. It should never go farther from your feet than the length of the string. Couple quick changes of speed and direction with deceptive foot and body movements to unbalance opponents and create additional space in which to dribble and maneuver with the ball (see Figure 2.1).

| FIGURE 2.1 | **KEYS TO SUCCESS** |

DRIBBLE FOR CLOSE CONTROL

Preparation	**Execution**	**Follow-Through**
1. Knees flexed ___	1. Focus on the ball ___	1. Maintain close control ___
2. Crouched position ___	2. Use body feints and deceptive foot movements ___	2. Accelerate away from opponent ___
3. Low center of gravity ___	3. Control ball with appropriate surface of foot ___	3. Look up and watch the field ___
4. Body over ball ___	4. Change speed, direction, or both ___	
5. Head up when possible ___		

Dribble for Speed

In some situations you don't have to be as concerned about dribbling for close control. For example, you may receive a pass in the open area between the opposing team's midfielders and defenders. Or you may find yourself with the ball in a breakaway situation behind the opponent's defense. In these instances you must be able to dribble at top speed. Rather than keeping the ball close to your feet, push it several feet ahead into the open space, sprint to it, and then push it again. Use your full instep or outside surface of your instep to push the ball forward (see Figure 2.2).

FIGURE 2.2	KEYS TO SUCCESS

DRIBBLE FOR SPEED

Preparation

1. Upright posture ___
2. Ball at your feet ___
3. Head up for good field vision ___

Execution

1. Focus on the ball ___
2. Contact ball with full instep or outside surface of instep ___
3. Push ball ahead several feet ___

Follow-Through

1. Head up for good field vision ___
2. Accelerate to the ball ___
3. Push ball ahead ___

Shielding

Proper positioning of your body in relation to the ball and a challenging opponent is very important. Position sideways, assume a slightly crouched posture, and control the ball with the foot farthest from the opponent. In the crouched position you have a wide base of support and can create greater distance be-tween the opponent and the ball. Use body feints, deceptive foot movements, and sudden changes of direction to unbalance the defender. Remember that the ball should always be within your range of control when shielding it from an opponent. If not, the referee can penalize you for unfairly obstructing the opponent (see Figure 2.3).

FIGURE 2.3 **KEYS TO SUCCESS**

SHIELDING

Preparation	Execution	Follow-Through
1. Close control of ball ___	1. Control ball with foot farthest from opponent ___	1. Readjust body position in response to opponent ___
2. Position sideways ___	2. Control ball with outside, inside, or sole of foot ___	2. Maintain low center of gravity ___
3. Crouched posture with knees flexed ___	3. Maintain wide base of support ___	3. Maintain space between ball and opponent ___
4. Arms out to sides for balance ___	4. Alternate vision from ball to opponent ___	
5. Head up and watch your opponent ___	5. Use body feints to unbalance opponent ___	
	6. Use deceptive foot movements ___	
	7. Use quick changes of direction ___	

DRIBBLING AND SHIELDING SUCCESS STOPPERS

Because the techniques used when dribbling for close control differ from those used when dribbling for speed, performance errors also differ. Even slight errors in judgment or technique may result in loss of possession when dribbling in a crowd of opponents. The margin for error is not so precise when dribbling in open space.

Most shielding errors are due to incorrect positioning of the body in relation to the ball and opponent. It is important to maintain as much space as possible between the ball and your challenger. To do so you must constantly readjust your position in response to the defender's movements. Common dribbling and shielding errors are discussed here along with suggestions for correcting them.

Error	Correction
Dribble for Close Control	
1. The ball rolls too far from your feet, out of your range of control.	1. Keep the ball beneath your body, as close to your feet as possible. From that position you can change direction quickly, and the ball is always within your immediate control. Develop a soft touch to control the ball smoothly as you dribble.
2. The ball gets tangled between your feet when you attempt to dribble.	2. Don't be too fancy or attempt too many different body movements when taking on an opponent. Become comfortable and proficient with a few dribbling moves and use those to beat opponents.
3. You quickly change direction and dribble directly into a defending opponent.	3. This may happen if you are looking down at the ball and are not aware of your immediate surroundings. Keep your head up as much as possible when dribbling. Good field vision is just as important as maintaining close control of the ball.
Dribble for Speed	
1. You feel awkward when dribbling the ball in open space.	1. The most natural method of pushing the ball forward when dribbling at speed is by using the outside surface of your instep. Extend your kicking foot down and inward as you contact the ball. Do not use the inside surface of your foot to push the ball forward because you cannot maintain a fluid, comfortable running motion using that technique.
2. You take short, choppy steps and have difficulty dribbling at speed.	2. Push the ball several feet ahead and then sprint to it. Do not touch the ball every step or two as you would when dribbling for close control.

Error	Correction
Shielding	
1. An opponent steals the ball from you.	1. Maintain as much distance as possible between the ball and your opponent. Position sideways to the defender in a slightly crouched stance. Spread your feet approximately shoulder-width apart and control the ball with the foot farthest from the opponent.
2. You are easily knocked off the ball by a legal shoulder charge from an opponent.	2. Poor balance, commonly referred to as a "lack of strength on the ball," usually results from standing too erect with feet close together. Maintain a crouched posture with feet approximately shoulder-width apart and weight centered. Good balance is essential.

How to Execute Tackling Skills

As we discussed earlier, your team won't score any goals when the other team has the ball. One method of regaining possession is by tackling the ball from an opponent. Become familiar with three basic tackling techniques: the block, the poke, and the slide tackle. Successful execution of each requires proper technique, precise timing of the challenge, good judgment, and confidence.

Block Tackle

Use the block tackle when an opponent is dribbling directly at you. Quickly close the distance to the dribbler. As you do so, position your feet in a staggered stance with one foot slightly ahead of the other. Assume a slightly crouched stance with knees flexed and arms out to the sides for balance. From this posture you will be able to react quickly to the dribbler's sudden movements or changes of direction. Tackle the ball by blocking it with the inside surface of your foot. Position your foot sideways and keep it firm as you drive it into the ball. You must play the ball, not the opponent, when tackling. If the referee judges that you are intentionally playing the person, you will be signaled for a rule violation (see Figure 2.4).

Poke Tackle

Use the poke tackle when you are approaching an opponent from the side or from slightly behind. As you near the dribbler, reach in with your leg, extend your foot, and poke the ball away with your toes. Remember to play the ball, not the opponent. Kicking your opponent while trying to set the ball free is a foul (see Figure 2.5).

Slide Tackle

The slide tackle is generally used as a last resort when an opponent has beaten you on the dribble and there is little hope of catching him or her. At that point your only course of action is to slide and kick the ball away in any direction possible.

You will use the slide tackle most often when approaching a dribbler from behind. The technique looks quite similar to that of a baseball player sliding into a base. Leave your feet as you near the ball and slide on your side to a position slightly ahead of the dribbler. At the same time snap your lower (sliding) leg straight and kick the ball away using the instep of your foot. Use the slide tackle sparingly. Because you must leave your feet to challenge for the ball, you are in a poor position to recover from a missed tackle (see Figure 2.6).

FIGURE 2.4   **KEYS TO SUCCESS**

BLOCK TACKLE

Preparation

1. Close distance to dribbler ___
2. Assume staggered stance ___
3. Crouched posture with weight balanced ___
4. Draw back blocking foot/leg ___
5. Position blocking foot sideways ___
6. Keep blocking foot firm ___
7. Focus on the ball ___

Execution

1. Shoulders square to dribbler ___
2. Shift momentum forward ___
3. Drive blocking foot through center of ball ___
4. Keep blocking foot firm ___
5. Maintain low center of gravity ___

Follow-Through

1. Momentum through point of contact ___
2. Push ball forward past opponent ___
3. Gain possession ___
4. Initiate counterattack ___

FIGURE 2.5

POKE TACKLE

Preparation

1. Close distance to dribbler ___
2. Assume slight crouch with knees flexed ___
3. Maintain balance and body control ___
4. Focus on the ball ___

Execution

1. Extend tackling leg/foot toward ball ___
2. Flex balance leg ___
3. Poke ball with toes ___
4. Avoid contact with dribbler prior to tackle ___

Follow-Through

1. Withdraw leg ___
2. Chase and collect ball ___

FIGURE 2.6 **KEYS TO SUCCESS**

SLIDE TACKLE

Preparation

1. Approach from behind or side ___
2. Assume crouched position as you near dribbler ___
3. Maintain balance and body control ___
4. Focus on the ball ___

Execution

1. Leave feet ___
2. Slide on side ___
3. Place arms to sides for balance ___
4. Extend sliding (lower) leg ahead of the ball ___
5. Extend tackling foot ___
6. Flex opposite leg at knee ___
7. Snap sliding leg/foot into ball ___
8. Contact ball on instep ___
9. Avoid contact with dribbler prior to tackle ___

Follow-Through

1. Jump to feet ___
2. Collect ball if possible ___

TACKLING SKILLS SUCCESS STOPPERS

In my thirty years as a player, coach, and camp director, I've observed very few players who possess good tackling skills. This is partly because tackling skills are difficult to master and also because they aren't practiced as often as they should be. Granted, it may be more fun to practice shooting or dribbling skills, but you won't get a chance to use those skills in match situations unless you first gain possession of the ball.

Most tackling errors result from poor timing of the challenge, lack of body control, or improper technique. You must maintain a low center of gravity, get close to the dribbler, and then tackle the ball with power and determination. Here is a list of common errors and suggested methods of correcting them.

Error	Correction
Block Tackle	
1. You block the ball but fail to gain possession.	1. Keep your body compact and in a crouched position. Block the ball with a short, powerful snap of your leg as you transfer your weight forward through the point of contact. Tackle with power and determination. Do not lean back and extend your leg as you tackle. In that position you are susceptible to injury and, should you miss the tackle, will be unable to recover quickly to chase the dribbler.
2. You dive in and miss the tackle.	2. Don't overcommit to the dribbler. Quickly close the distance between yourself and the dribbler, wait for an opportune moment, and then tackle with confidence and determination.
Poke Tackle	
1. You foul the dribbler when attempting to tackle the ball.	1. Don't be fooled by the dribbler's body movements. Close the distance to the dribbler, get a clear view of the ball, and then extend your leg and foot to poke the ball away.
Slide Tackle	
1. You slide from behind into the dribbler.	1. Do not initiate your slide from directly behind the dribbler. Slide past him or her and then attempt to hook your leg around from the side to kick the ball away. Remember, you have committed a foul if you initiate contact with the dribbler without first touching the ball.

DRILLS

1. Individual Dribble

Dribble in random fashion within a large field area. Use various surfaces of your foot to control the ball. Incorporate changes of direction and speed into your dribbling pattern. For example, quickly change direction by cutting the ball with the instep of your right foot, then accelerate into open space by pushing the ball with the outside of your left foot. Begin the exercise at a jog and gradually increase speed. Imagine that there are opposing players all around you, so emphasize close control of the ball. If teammates are available, dribble among yourselves. Dribble continuously until you have touched the ball 200 times with various surfaces of your feet.

Success Goal = 200 touches keeping the ball within range of control ___

Success Check
• Close control ___
• Low center of gravity ___
• Sudden changes of speed and direction ___

To Increase Difficulty
• Dribble in a confined area with several teammates.
• Increase dribbling speed to simulate game conditions.
• Change both speed and direction with each touch of the ball.

To Decrease Difficulty
• Reduce the number of touches to 100.
• Reduce dribbling speed.

2. Slalom Dribble

Pair with a teammate. Set up a line of six cones spaced 2 yards apart. Begin at the first cone and dribble in and out of the cones until you get to the last one, then turn and dribble in and out of the cones back to the starting line. Keep the ball under close control at all times and complete the slalom as quickly as possible. Exchange the ball with your teammate and rest while he or she dribbles the circuit. Repeat the slalom dribble course 20 times each. Knocking down a cone is a dribbling error. Award yourself one point for each complete circuit through the cones without error.

Success Goal = 18 of a possible 20 points ___

Success Check
• Maintain balance and body control ___
• Close ball control ___
• Head up as much as possible ___

To Increase Difficulty
• Position cones 1 yard apart.
• Increase number of cones.

To Decrease Difficulty
• Increase distance between cones to 3 yards.
• Reduce number of cones.
• Dribble at half speed.

3. Speed Dribble Relay

Select two teammates to participate with you in this exercise. You and one teammate position on the goal line while the other teammate positions on the edge of the penalty area (18-yard line) facing you. Begin the relay by dribbling at top speed to the edge of the penalty area and exchanging possession of the ball with the teammate positioned there. You remain at that spot while he or she dribbles the ball back to the goal line and exchanges possession with the third player who continues the relay by dribbling the ball back to you. Continue the relay until each player has dribbled 20 lengths of the penalty area. Award yourself one point for each time you dribble the 18-yard distance and exchange possession of the ball with a teammate without error. An error occurs if the ball bounces out of your range of control as you exchange possession with a teammate.

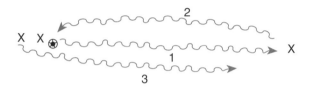

Success Goal = 18 of 20 possible points ___

Success Check
- Push ball ahead with outside of instep ___
- Sprint to ball and push again ___
- Slow down when exchanging possession ___

To Increase Difficulty
- Increase dribbling distance.
- Increase repetitions to 30.
- Add an extra player who chases the dribbler from behind.

To Decrease Difficulty
- Decrease dribbling distance.
- Perform drill at half speed.

4. Block Tackle Stationary Ball

Face a teammate standing 3 yards away who pins a ball to the ground with his or her foot while you practice the block-tackle technique on the stationary ball. Move toward the ball, firmly position your blocking foot sideways, and block tackle the ball with the inside surface of your foot. Execute 25 block tackles with each foot. Award yourself one point for each correct repetition of the block-tackle technique.

 **Success Goal** =

25 correct repetitions with right foot ___
25 correct repetitions with left foot ___

Success Check

- Crouched posture with knees flexed ___
- Low center of gravity ___
- Weight balanced ___

To Increase Difficulty

- Increase speed of repetition.
- Block tackle ball from teammate who is slowly dribbling at you.

To Decrease Difficulty

- Walk through the drill.
- Use only favorite foot to block the ball.

5. Tackle the Dribbler

A teammate dribbles at you from a distance of 10 yards. Quickly move forward to close the distance to the dribbler, assume a proper defensive posture, and attempt to block tackle the ball. You may tackle with either foot depending upon the dribbler's angle of approach. Repeat the drill 20 times, then switch roles with your teammate. Award yourself one point for each successful block tackle.

 **Success Goal** = 16 of 20 possible points ___

Success Check

- Maintain low center of gravity ___
- Balance and body control ___
- Keep blocking foot firm ___
- Contact center of ball ___

 **To Increase Difficulty**

- Increase distance to 15 yards.

To Decrease Difficulty

- Reduce distance to 5 yards.
- Require dribbler to advance at half speed.

6. Cone to Cone

Position two cones approximately 10 yards apart along a sideline or endline of the field. Stand with a ball on one side of the line midway between the cones while a teammate (defender) faces you without a ball on the opposite side of the line. Your objective is to dribble the ball laterally to one cone or the other before the defender can get there. The defender tries to react instantly to your every move so you don't beat him or her to a cone with the ball. Use body feints, deceptive foot movements, and quick changes of speed and direction to unbalance the defender. Neither player is allowed to cross the line at any time during the drill. You win one point each time that you dribble and stop the ball at a cone before the defender can establish position there. Play for 2 minutes, rest, then switch roles and play again. Play a total of 10 games, 5 as the dribbler and 5 as defender.

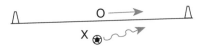

Success Goal = Score five points in each 2-minute game when playing as the dribbler ___

Success Check

Dribbler:
- Keep ball in close control ___
- Sudden changes of speed and direction ___
- Deceptive body feints ___

Defender:
- Maintain low center of gravity ___
- Balance and body control ___
- Focus on the ball ___

To Increase Difficulty
- Increase distance between cones to 15 yards.

To Decrease Difficulty
- Decrease distance between cones to 5 yards.

7. Line-to-Line Game

Compete against an opponent within a 10-by-20-yard grid. Position yourself with a ball on one endline of the grid while the opponent stations on the opposite endline. Serve the ball to your opponent who receives it and immediately attempts to dribble the length of the grid. Your objective is to prevent him or her from dribbling past your endline. Play at game speed. Use either the block-tackle or poke-tackle techniques to dispossess the dribbler. You earn two points for a successful block tackle and one point for each time you dispossess the dribbler using the poke tackle. Award the dribbler one point for dribbling the ball past you over your endline. Return to your respective starting points after each attempt. Repeat 20 times, then switch roles so your opponent can practice his or her tackling skills. The player scoring the most points wins.

Success Goal = Score more points than opponent ___

Success Check

Dribbler:
- Deceptive body feints ___
- Sudden changes of speed ___
- Close control ___

Defender:
- Weight balanced ___
- Low center of gravity ___
- Focus on the ball ___
- Don't overcommit ___

 To Increase Difficulty

(for Defender)
- Increase field width so dribbler has more space in which to maneuver.
- Place two small goals on endline behind defender to provide dribbler with additional scoring options.

To Decrease Difficulty

(for Defender)
- Reduce field width to decrease available space for the dribbler.

8. Individual Ball Possession Game

Maintain possession of the ball from a teammate within a 12-by-12-yard grid. The teammate applies only passive pressure and does not actually try to tackle the ball. Play for 90 seconds. Penalize yourself one point for each time the ball leaves the grid or each time it rolls outside of your range of control. Play five rounds with a short rest between each, then switch roles and play five more rounds.

Success Goal = Fewer than 15 penalty points in five 90-second rounds ___

Success Check
- Position sideways between ball and opponent ___
- Control ball with foot farthest from opponent ___
- Quick changes of speed and direction ___
- Move away from defensive pressure ___

 To Increase Difficulty
- Decrease grid size.
- Lengthen rounds to 120 seconds each.
- Require defender to apply maximum pressure in attempt to win the ball.

To Decrease Difficulty
- Increase grid size.
- Shorten rounds to 60 seconds.

9. All Versus All

Play this game with several friends. Each player has a ball and stations within the center circle of the soccer field. Use dribbling and shielding skills to maintain possession of your ball. At the same time attempt to tackle and kick other players' balls out of the circle. Use block or poke tackles only; slide tackles are not permitted due to the potential for injury in a crowded area. Award yourself one point for each ball that you tackle and kick out of the circle. Penalize yourself one point for each time your ball is kicked out of the circle. Quickly retrieve your ball if it is kicked out of the circle and return to play. Play for 5 minutes and keep a total of your points.

 **Success Goal** = Score the most points ___

Success Check
• Close ball control ___
• Sudden changes of speed and direction ___
• Shield ball from opponents ___

 To Increase Difficulty
(for Dribblers)
• Reduce circle size.
• Add players to the game to reduce available space.

 To Decrease Difficulty
(for Dribblers)
• Increase circle size so dribblers have more space in which to maneuver.

10. Tackle All

Use markers to outline a field area approximately 30 yards square. Select a partner who stations with you outside of the area without soccer balls. You and your partner are the defenders. All remaining players, each with a ball, begin dribbling randomly within the field area. On command, the defenders sprint into the area and attempt to tackle and gain possession of a dribbler's ball. If you are successful, kick the ball out of the area and immediately try to steal another. Award yourself one point for each ball that you kick out of the area. A dribbler who loses his or her ball is eliminated from the game. He or she must retrieve the ball and practice ball juggling outside of the playing area. The game ends when all dribblers have been eliminated. Whoever (you or your partner) totals the most points wins the game. Repeat the game with two different defenders.

Success Goal = Score more points than your partner when playing as a defender ___

Success Check
• Maintain balance and body control ___
• Low center of gravity ___
• Tackle with power and determination ___

 To Increase Difficulty
(for Defenders)
• Increase size of playing area.
• Increase the number of dribblers.

To Decrease Difficulty
(for Defenders)
• Reduce size of playing area.
• Reduce the number of dribblers.

11. Attack or Defend

Divide into two teams of four or five players. Use markers to outline a 30-by-40-yard playing area bisected by a midline. Distribute soccer balls, one ball for every two players, evenly along the midline. Teams position on opposite endlines with players spread an equal distance apart. On command, players from both teams sprint to the midline, compete for possession of a ball, and attempt to dribble it back to their own endline. Award one team point for each ball returned over an endline. Players who fail to gain possession of a ball try to prevent opponents from scoring by tackling their balls and kicking them out of the area. The round ends when all balls have been returned over an endline or kicked out of the area. Play 10 rounds with a short rest between each. The team scoring the most points after 10 rounds wins the game.

 **Success Goal** = Score the most points ___

Success Check
• Be first to a ball ___
• Protect ball by shielding ___
• Dribble at top speed ___

To Increase Difficulty
• Narrow the field area to reduce available dribbling space.

To Decrease Difficulty
• Increase size of playing area.

12. Game With Restricted Dribbling

Divide into two teams of four or five players. Use markers to outline a 60-by-40-yard field with a 5-yard-wide goal on each endline. Divide the field lengthwise into three equal-size zones. Station one player from each team as a goalkeeper. Begin with a kickoff from the center of the field. Score goals by kicking the ball through the opponent's goal. Regular soccer rules apply except for the following zone restrictions:

• Players may use only one- and two-touch passes in the zone nearest their goal.
• In the central zone players may dribble to advance the ball into open space, but may not take on and beat opponents.
• Dribbling is mandatory in the attacking third of the field. In this zone players must beat an opponent by dribbling before passing to a teammate or shooting on goal.

Violation of a zone restriction is penalized by loss of possession to the opponents.

Success Goal = Score more goals than opponents ___

Success Check
• Close ball control ___
• Sudden changes of speed and direction ___
• Head up and watch the field ___

To Increase Difficulty
(for Attacking Team)
• Reduce field area to restrict the space and time available.
• Add one neutral player who always plays with the defending team to give that team a numerical advantage.

To Decrease Difficulty
(for Attacking Team)
• Increase field area to provide dribblers more space in which to maneuver.
• Add one neutral player who always plays with the attacking team to give that team a numerical advantage.
• Don't use goalkeepers.

13. Score by Dribbling Only

Divide into two teams of three or four players. Play on a field area of approximately 50 by 35 yards. Each team defends an endline. Regular soccer rules apply except for the method of scoring. Goals are scored by dribbling the ball over the opponent's endline rather than by shooting. The entire length of the endline is the goal line. Award one team point each time a player dribbles the ball over the opponent's endline. Play for 25 minutes and keep track of points. The team scoring the most points wins.

Success Goal = Score the most points ___

Success Check

When Attacking:
• Maintain close control of ball ___
• Quick changes of speed and direction ___
• Take on opponents in attacking third ___

When Defending:
• Maintain balance and body control ___
• Do not overcommit ___
• Prevent penetration by dribbler ___

To Increase Difficulty

(for Attacking Team)
• Decrease area width to limit available space.
• Add two neutral players who always play with the defending team to give that team a numerical advantage.

To Decrease Difficulty

(for Attacking Team)
• Increase area size to provide more space to maneuver.
• Add two neutral players who always play with the attacking team to give that team a numerical advantage.

SUCCESS SUMMARY

A good dribbler is not necessarily being a ball hog. If you use your dribbling skills to best advantage—to penetrate opposing defenses and take on defenders at opportune times—you will greatly improve your team's ability to attack and score goals. Dribbling skills are fun to practice. All you need is a ball and an open field area. Ask your coach, a parent, or a teammate to observe as you combine dribbling and shielding skills in practice and game situations. The observer should pay particular attention to your balance and body control, how quickly you can change speed and direction, the effectiveness of your body feints and deceptive foot movements, and how you position your body to protect the ball from a challenging opponent. The observer should always keep in mind that dribbling is an individual art that can be expressed in different ways. He or she can use the checklists in Figures 2.1, 2.2, and 2.3 to evaluate your overall performance and provide helpful hints for improvement.

Your coach or a teammate can also watch you execute the block-, poke-, and slide-tackle techniques in practice and game situations. He or she can use the checklists in Figures 2.4, 2.5, and 2.6 to evaluate your performance.

STEP

3

INDIVIDUAL ATTACK AND DEFENSE TACTICS: GOING ONE-ON-ONE

A soccer game is 90 minutes of flowing action. The typical match is a series of constantly changing situations, each lasting only a few moments before blending into the next. Your ability to make good decisions, to do the "right thing" in a given situation, is just as important as the ability to execute soccer skills. You can improve your decisions by understanding the basic concepts of attack and defense tactics. It is best to start with the simplest tactical unit, that is, one player versus one player.

Although soccer is ultimately a team game, every match includes a series of one-on-one confrontations. These minicompetitions waged between opposing players are links in the chain of events that determine the final outcome of the game. As the saying goes: A chain is only as strong as its weakest link. Don't be the weak link in your team. Develop your ability to perform successfully in one-on-one situations.

Why Are Individual Attacking and Defending Tactics Important?

Soccer, much like basketball and hockey, requires that all field players be able to defend as well as attack. When you have possession of the ball, you are the attacker; when your opponent has the ball, you are the defender. Success in one-on-one situations depends in part on your ability to choose the best course of action from a multitude of options. If you consistently make poor decisions, you will probably

lose more individual matchups than you win, and your team will suffer the consequences.

How to Execute Individual Attack Tactics

When you have the ball, base your decisions on the following guidelines. Progress through the sequence of steps in the order listed.

Maintain Ball Possession

First and foremost, you must not lose possession of the ball to an opponent. Obviously your team cannot score without the ball, and each loss of possession gives the opposing team a potential scoring opportunity. Use your dribbling and shielding skills to protect the ball from challengers (see Figure 3.1).

Create Space for Yourself

In soccer an important equation always holds true: *Space equals time.* The more the space between you and the marking opponent, the more time you will have to execute skills, make decisions, and play the ball. You become a better player simply by creating space for yourself.

You can create space between yourself and a marking opponent with deceptive body feints and checking runs. *Body feints* are movements designed to mislead, or unbalance, the opponent. A slight dip of your shoulder or a quick step over the ball may be all you need to get your opponent to lean the wrong way (see Figure 3.2). A *checking run* is a short, quick fore, you must position yourself to go forward whenever possible. For example, at times you may receive a ball while positioned with your back to the opponents' goal. In this situation, because you are facing your own goal, the advantage still lies with the defending player. You can shift the advantage to your favor by turning with the ball to face the opponent. Before attempting to turn you must first create space between yourself and the marking defender (see Figure 3.3).

Take on the Defender

Dribble directly at the defender once you have turned with the ball. This action is commonly referred to as *taking on* a defender and forces the defender to make a decision: either commit to tackle the ball or retreat in an attempt to delay penetration. If the defender makes the wrong decision, you may find yourself with a scoring opportunity.

Take on an opponent only in certain areas of the field. Always weigh the risk of losing possession versus the potential reward of creating a scoring opportunity. Think safety first in your own end of the field. Do not take on an opponent in the defending third of the field nearest your own goal. Loss of possession there can be costly; it may result in a goal against your team. You can use dribbling skills to best advantage in the attacking third of the field nearest the opponent's goal. Loss of possession in that area is

Figure 3.1   Position your body to maintain ball possession.

Figure 3.2   Body feints are one way to create space for yourself.

burst of speed designed to fool the defender into thinking that you are going to run past him or her. Use checking runs to create space in which to receive a pass from a teammate. Accelerate forward a couple of steps as if you are going to run behind the defender, then suddenly check back toward your teammate to receive the ball.

Turn on the Defender

Your ultimate objective is to score goals or create opportunities for teammates to score goals. There-

Figure 3.3   Create space first, then turn on your opponent.

not as critical, and the potential reward for beating an opponent on the dribble is to score a goal.

Take the Shortest Route to the Goal

Follow the most direct route to the goal. Once you have beaten a defender on the dribble, don't let him or her catch you. You should never have to pass the same defender twice on your way to the goal.

How to Execute Individual Defense Tactics

An attacker may be willing to risk possession loss in certain situations in an attempt to create a goal-scoring opportunity. A defender, on the other hand, can't afford to take risks when attempting to win the ball because even a small miscalculation can result in an opponent's score. Your objective as a defender is to keep the play in front of you, to prevent the opponent from penetrating with a pass or dribble. As with individual attacking tactics, the decisions you make will play a critical role in your overall performance. Use the following principles to guide your actions when defending in a one-on-one situation.

Goalside Position

Your position in relation to the opponent, the ball, and your goal is very important. Always position *goalside*, between the opponent you are marking and the goal you are defending. From here you can keep both the ball and opponent in view at all times. It is also to your advantage to position slightly to the inside of the opponent, shading him or her toward the center of the field. From there you can shut off the dribbler's most direct route to goal.

Approach to the Ball

Quickly close the distance to the opponent you are marking when you see that he or she is about to receive the ball. Ideally you should arrive at the scene about the same moment as the ball does. Slow your approach as you near the opponent to maintain optimal balance and body control. Remember the important equation we discussed earlier: Space equals time. The less space you allow for your opponent to receive and control the ball, the less time he or she will have to make decisions and play the ball.

Defensive Stance

Assume a slightly crouched posture with knees flexed and a low center of gravity (see Figure 3.4). Use a staggered stance with feet a comfortable distance apart and one foot slightly forward. From this position you can quickly change direction in response to the opponent's movements. With feet in a staggered position, you can also prevent the opponent from pushing the ball between your legs, a dribbling maneuver commonly referred to as the "nutmeg." Being nutmeged is the ultimate embarrassment for a defending player.

Marking Distance

How tightly should you mark an opponent when defending in a one-on-one situation? Base your decision on the following:

• *Ability of the opponent.* Give the opponent a bit more space if he or she has great speed and quickness. This will prevent him or her from merely pushing the ball forward and outracing you. Mark more tightly if your opponent relies on a high degree of skill rather than quickness. Deny him or her adequate time and space to use those skills to beat you.

• *Area of the field.* As a general rule, the closer the opponent is to your goal, the tighter he or she should be marked. An opponent within scoring range of your goal must be denied the opportunity to shoot or pass the ball forward.

Figure 3.4 Assume a defensive posture: flexed knees, staggered stance, vision focused on the ball.

• *Position of the ball in relation to opponent.* Allow your opponent more space as he or she moves farther away from the position of the ball. The marking distance should be such that if the ball is passed to him or her you can close the space while the ball is in flight. Always position yourself so that the ball and the opponent you are marking are within sight.

Control and Balance

A dribbler will use deceptive body feints and foot movements to unbalance you, to get you leaning one way or another. Strive to maintain good balance and body control at all times. Keep your weight centered over the balls of your feet. Don't lean back on your heels and don't challenge for the ball in a reckless manner.

Prevent the Turn

Try to prevent your opponent from turning with the ball to face your goal. Once turned, he or she will be able to serve penetrating passes into the space behind you or attempt to beat you on the dribble. Your marking should be tight, but not so tight that the attacker can spin with the ball and roll off of you. Always be in position to see the ball and be ready to step forward to block tackle the ball as your opponent attempts to turn.

Containment

If by some weird quirk of fate an opponent does successfully turn on you with the ball, your immediate priority is to deny penetration. Channel the opponent into areas where space is limited (e.g., toward the sideline or into a nearby teammate), or force him or her to pass the ball square or back toward his or her own goal. If you can delay penetration via the pass or dribble, even for a few moments, your teammates will have time to recover to positions goalside of the ball to support you in defense.

Tackle the Ball

If you sense that the opponent has allowed the ball to get too far from his or her control, tackle hard and gain possession of the ball.

INDIVIDUAL ATTACK AND DEFENSE SUCCESS STOPPERS

Because individual tactics focus on what to do and when to do it, most errors that occur are due to poor judgment. Regardless of how skilled or talented you may be, you won't enjoy much success if you consistently make the wrong decisions in one-on-one situations. Common errors are listed here along with suggestions for avoiding or correcting them.

Error	Correction
Individual Attack Tactics	
1. The defender kicks the ball away from you.	1. Position your body to shield the ball at all times.
2. You lose the ball when attempting to turn on the defender.	2. Use body feints, checking movements, or sudden changes of direction to create space between yourself and the marking defender. Don't turn with the ball without first creating space in which to turn.
3. You hesitate in taking on the marking defender, which gives other defenders time to recover goalside of the ball.	3. Be decisive. After turning with the ball, dribble immediately at the defending player to commit him or her.

Error	Correction
Individual Defense Tactics	
1. Your opponent turns with the ball to face you.	1. Tight marking is essential. Deny your opponent space to turn with the ball.
2. Your opponent passes the ball forward into the space behind you.	2. This can occur if your marking distance is too great. Step forward to close the gap and apply immediate pressure on the ball. This action forces the attacker to pass the ball square or back to a supporting teammate rather than forward and will give your teammates time to recover to a position goalside of the ball.
3. You overcommit in an effort to tackle the ball and are beaten on the dribble.	3. Your first priority in a one-on-one situation is to prevent penetration, not to gain possession of the ball. Position feet in a staggered stance and distribute weight evenly. Maintain balance and body control at all times. You should challenge for the ball only when a teammate is covering the space immediately behind you, when you are relatively sure you can successfully execute the tackle, or both.

INDIVIDUAL ATTACK AND DEFENSE TACTICS

DRILLS

1. Keep Away

Play against a teammate within a 10-by-20-yard area. You begin with possession of the ball while your teammate plays as the defender. Use sudden changes of speed and direction, coupled with dribbling and shielding skills, to keep the ball from your teammate. Play for 15 seconds, rest for 30 seconds, and repeat. Award yourself one point each time you can maintain possession of the ball for a 15-second round. Award the defender one point each time he or she steals the ball or kicks it out of the playing area. Play 10 rounds as the attacker, then switch roles and play 10 rounds as the defender.

Success Goal =

6 or more points as attacker ___
6 or more points as defender ___

Success Check

Attacker:
• Position body to shield the ball ___
• Maintain space between ball and defender ___
• Use sudden changes of speed and direction ___

Defender:
• Maintain balance and body control ___
• Limit space available to attacker ___
• Prevent the turn ___

To Increase Difficulty

(for Attacker)
• Award one point for a 20-second possession time.
• Decrease size of playing area.

To Decrease Difficulty

(for Attacker)
• Award one point for a 10-second possession time.
• Require defender to play at 50% effort.
• Increase size of playing area.

2. Receive and Control Under Pressure

Play with two teammates within a 10-by-20-yard area. Position near one endline of the area; a teammate positions 2 yards behind you as a marking defender. The third player acts as a server and positions at the opposite end of the area with a supply of soccer balls. Receive a rolling ball from the server while the defender challenges you from behind. Shield the ball from the defender as you receive it. Try to maintain possession of the ball from the defender for a 10-second round, then return it to the server. Repeat 10 rounds. Award yourself one point if you can maintain possession of the ball within the area for 10 seconds. Award the defender one point each time he or she tackles the ball from you. Players rotate positions after 10 rounds. Continue until each player has taken a turn as the defender and the attacker.

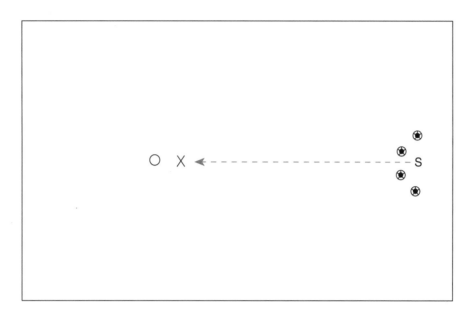

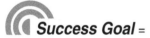 **Success Goal** =

7 or more points as attacker ___
7 or more points as defender ___

 **Success Check**

Attacker:
• Check toward ball ___
• Shield ball with body ___
• Maintain close control ___

Defender:
• Tight marking ___
• Focus on the ball ___
• Prevent the turn ___

 To Increase Difficulty

(for Attacker)
• Decrease size of playing area.
• Receive and control lofted passes.
• Award one point for a 15-second possession time.
• Require attacker to turn on defender within 10 seconds.

To Decrease Difficulty

(for Attacker)
• Increase size of playing area.
• Award one point for a 5-second possession time.

3. Turn and Take on the Defender

The drill proceeds in the same manner as the preceding one. You win one point each time you turn with the ball to face the defender and one additional point if you beat the defender by dribbling past him or her to the endline of the 10-by-20-yard area. You have 10 seconds once you receive the ball to turn and take on the defender. Award the defender 2 points if he or she prevents you from turning with the ball within the 10-second limit and 1 point if he or she tackles the ball as you attempt to dribble past. Play 10 rounds for a maximum possible total of 20 points each, then switch roles and repeat for 10 more rounds. Continue until each player has taken a turn as the defender and the attacker.

Success Goal =

12 or more points as attacker ___
14 or more points as defender ___

✔ **Success Check**

Attacker:
• Check to ball ___
• Shield ball with body ___
• Create space to turn ___

Defender:
• Close space as attacker receives ball ___
• Maintain balance and body control ___
• Anticipate attacker's movements ___

 To Increase Difficulty

(for Attacker)
• Receive and control lofted passes from server.
• Reduce size of playing area to limit attacking space.

To Decrease Difficulty

(for Attacker)
• Position defender 5 yards behind attacker.
• Require defender to play at half speed.

4. One-on-One to a Central Goal

Play against a teammate within an area approximately 20 yards square. Place two cones 2 yards apart near the center of the area to represent a common goal. You begin with possession of the ball. Your objective is to beat the opponent and pass the ball through either side of the central goal. Award yourself one point for each goal scored. Loss of possession occurs when the defender steals the ball, when the ball travels outside of the area, and after each goal scored. Play nonstop for 5 minutes. Players alternate from attack to defense with each change of possession. The player scoring the most points wins the game.

 **Success Goal** = Score the most points ___

✔ **Success Check**

Attacker:
• Protect the ball ___
• Turn when possible ___
• Take on defender ___

Defender:
• Maintain goalside position ___
• Balance and body control ___
• Tackle with authority ___

 To Increase Difficulty
• Position two goals within the area.
• Play for 10 minutes nonstop.

To Decrease Difficulty
• Shorten playing time to 3 minutes.
• Increase goal size.

5. Defend the Line

Play one-on-one with a teammate. Position cones or flags to represent a 4-yard-wide goal. Stand on the goal line with a ball while your teammate faces you at a distance of 25 yards. To begin, serve a lofted pass to your teammate, then move forward off the goal line to play as a defender. Your teammate controls the ball and attempts to dribble past you through the goal. Award yourself one point if you successfully tackle and gain possession of the ball; award the attacker one point if he or she dribbles past you through the goal. Play 20 rounds as the defender, then switch roles and play 20 rounds as the attacker.

Success Goal = Score the most points __

Success Check

Attacker:
• Take on defender at speed __
• Use sudden changes of speed and direction __

Defender:
• Close distance to attacker __
• Maintain balance and body control __
• Maintain good defensive posture __
• Tackle at opportune moment __

To Increase Difficulty

(for Attacker)
• Use only two touches to receive and control the ball.
• Decrease goal width to 2 yards.

To Decrease Difficulty

(for Attacker)
• Increase goal width to 6 yards.
• Require defender to protect two goals.

6. Four-Zone Game

Play with three teammates. Use markers to divide a 10-by-40-yard area into four 10-by-10-yard zones. You position in Zone 1 with the ball; your teammates position respectively in Zones 2, 3, and 4 as defenders. Your objective is to dribble past the defender in each zone while staying within the side boundaries of the area. Defenders are restricted to movement within their assigned zone. If you take on and beat the defender in the first zone, immediately continue forward to take on the defender in the next zone. Award yourself one point for each defender beaten for a maximum of three points per round. If a defender steals the ball from you, he or she immediately returns it to you so you can move forward to take on the defender in the next zone.

After taking on the last defender in Zone 4, remain there to play as a defender for the next round. Each of the original defenders moves forward one zone. The player who moves into Zone 1 becomes the attacker for Round 2. Continue until each person has played five rounds as the attacker. The player with the most points wins the game.

Success Goal = Score the most points __

Success Check

Attacker:
• Use sudden changes of speed and direction __
• Use deceptive body feints to unbalance defender __
• Take on defender at speed __

Defender:
• Position feet in staggered stance __
• Maintain balance and body control __

To Increase Difficulty

(for Attacker)
• Decrease zone width to 5 yards.
• Increase number of zones and opponents to five.

To Decrease Difficulty

(for Attacker)
• Widen zones to 15 yards.
• Require defenders to play at half speed.

7. One Versus One With Minigoals

Play with two 2-player teams. Use markers to outline a rectangular playing area of 15 by 20 yards. One player on each team positions as a goal by standing with feet spread apart at the center of his or her endline. The other players station in the center of the area for one-on-one competition. Award one player the ball to begin.

Dribble past your opponent and pass the ball through the legs of the player positioned as a goal in order to score a goal. If your opponent steals the ball, he or she tries to score through your goal. Players positioned as goals must remain stationary and may not stop the ball from rolling through their legs. Change of possession occurs when the defending player steals the ball, when the ball travels out of play, and after each score.

Compete one-on-one for 3 minutes, then switch positions with your teammate (goalkeeper) and allow him or her to play one-on-one for 3 minutes while you rest. Play a total of ten rounds, alternating as a goalkeeper every other round. The coach or a goalkeeper keeps time. The team scoring the most points after ten rounds wins.

Success Goal = Score more points than opponents ___

Success Check

Attacker:
• Protect ball ___
• Turn on defender ___
• Take on defender ___

Defender:
• Maintain goalside position ___
• Feet positioned in staggered stance ___
• Maintain balance and body control ___

To Increase Difficulty
• Play 5-minute rounds.
• Increase field size.

To Decrease Difficulty
• Shorten rounds to 2 minutes.

8. Dribble the Gauntlet

Play with 6 to 10 teammates. Use markers to outline a rectangular field area of 20 by 35 yards with a 5-yard-deep safety zone at each end. You station in the center of the area without a ball as the "hunter." Your teammates, each with a ball, station in a safety zone at one end of the field. On command, all players leave their safety zone and attempt to dribble past you to the safety zone at the opposite end of the field. Try to prevent dribblers from reaching the opposite safety zone by tackling their balls and kicking them outside of the playing area. Award yourself one point for each ball you kick out of the area. Dribblers who reach the safety zone remain there until you give the command to return to the original safety zone.

A dribbler whose ball is kicked out of the area joins you as a hunter for the next round. Continue the game until all original dribblers become hunters. The last dribbler to lose possession of his or her ball becomes the first hunter in the next game. Repeat several times.

Success Goal = Score more points than other hunters ___

Success Check

Dribbler:
• Use sudden changes of speed and direction ___
• Maintain close ball control ___

Hunter:
• Maintain balance and body control ___
• Good defensive posture ___
• Tackle with power and determination ___

To Increase Difficulty

(for Hunters)
• Increase width of field area.

To Decrease Difficulty

(for Hunters)
• Narrow the field area.

9. One-on-One Marking Game

Divide into two teams of three players each. Use markers to outline a playing area of 25 by 40 yards with a goal 4 yards wide at the center of each endline. Do not use goalkeepers. Award one team possession of the ball.

Begin with a kickoff from the center of the field. Each team defends a goal. Require strict one-on-one marking of opponents. Regular soccer rules apply except that the offside law is waived. Because goalkeepers are not used and shots may be taken from anywhere on the field, marking must be very tight to prevent long-range goals. Change of possession occurs when a defending player steals the ball, when the ball goes out of play, or when a goal is scored. The team scoring the most goals wins the game.

Success Goal = Score more goals than opponents ___

Success Check

Defender:
• Maintain goalside position ___
• Knees flexed with low center of gravity ___
• Position to prevent penetration by pass or dribble ___

Attacker:
• Protect the ball ___
• Take on defender in attacking third of field ___
• Penetrate with a pass or dribble ___

To Increase Difficulty

(for Defenders)
• Increase size of playing area.
• Increase goal size.
• Place three small goals on endline to provide attackers with additional scoring options.

To Decrease Difficulty

(for Defenders)
• Reduce size of playing area.
• Reduce goal size.

SUCCESS SUMMARY

Practicing one-on-one tactics is challenging and fun. Most exercises are highly competitive, physically demanding, and test your ability to execute skills and make decisions under gamelike conditions. Get a group of teammates together and set up a mini one-on-one tournament where each player plays a game against every other player. Keep tally of wins and losses to determine a tournament winner. Have your coach or some other knowledgeable soccer person observe the tournament and analyze your performance. He or she can provide helpful advice that you can use to improve your one-on-one play. The observer should pay special attention to whether you are choosing the most appropriate action(s) for each situation.

STEP 4

HEADING SKILLS: PLAYING THE AIR GAME

When your soccer coach tells you to "use your head," he or she really means it! Soccer is the only game in which players use their heads to propel the ball. Players use the *jump header* to head (pass) the ball to a teammate, to score off a ball that crosses into an opponent's goal area, or to clear the ball out of their own goal area. The *dive header* is an exciting and acrobatic skill used only in special situations; for instance, to score spectacular goals off low crosses. Do not execute the dive header in a crowd of players, however. Someone may accidentally kick you in the face or head while trying to play the ball. Use good judgment!

Why Are Heading Skills Important?

Some teams rely on heading skills much more than others. For example, during the 1994 World Cup, teams from Norway and Ireland based their attacks on the ability of their forwards to win air balls. Both teams favored a long-pass-style game where balls were played through the air directly from the defenders to the forwards. In contrast, teams from Brazil, Mexico, and Colombia favored a short-passing, ball-control style of play with the ball on the ground much of the time.

Regardless of your team's style of play, it is inevitable that the ball is going to be in the air at various times during a game. To be a complete soccer player you must develop good heading skills. Goal kicks, corner kicks, lofted passes, and defensive clearances must often be played directly out of the air with your head.

How to Execute the Jump Header

Face the ball as it descends; keep your shoulders square. Use a two-footed takeoff to jump straight up. While in the air, arch your upper body back and tuck your chin toward your chest. Keep your neck firm and focus on the ball. Snap your upper trunk forward and contact the ball on the flat surface of your forehead at the highest point of your jump. Head the ball on a downward plane toward the goal line when attempting to score or to a teammate's feet when passing. Head the ball high, far, and wide, toward the flank area of the field, when clearing the ball from your own goal area. In all cases keep your eyes open and mouth closed as the ball contacts your head. Heading with your mouth open is inviting injury because you may bite your tongue if an opponent who is also jumping for the ball bumps you (see Figure 4.1).

How to Execute the Dive Header

Use the dive header to head a ball that is traveling parallel to the ground at waist level or lower. When possible, square your shoulders with the oncoming ball and assume a slightly crouched position. Judge the velocity of the ball, anticipate its arrival, and dive parallel to the ground to meet it. Tilt your head back—eyes open, mouth closed, and neck firm—as the ball contacts your forehead. Extend your arms downward to break your fall to the ground (see Figure 4.1).

FIGURE 4.1   **KEYS TO SUCCESS**

JUMP HEADER AND DIVE HEADER

Jump Header
Preparation

1. Square shoulders to oncoming ball ___
2. Flex knees ___
3. Keep weight on balls of feet ___
4. Draw arms back ___
5. Focus on the ball ___

Execution

6. Jump upward ___
7. Two-footed takeoff ___
8. Raise arms for upward momentum ___
9. Arch upper trunk ___
10. Tuck chin to chest ___
11. Neck firm ___
12. Snap upper trunk forward ___
13. Contact ball on forehead ___
14. Eyes open and mouth closed ___

Follow-Through

15. Drive forehead through point of contact with ball ___
16. Follow-through motion with upper trunk ___
17. Arms out to sides for balance ___
18. Land softly on ground with both feet ___

Dive Header
Preparation

1. Square shoulders to oncoming ball ___
2. Assume slightly crouched position ___
3. Keep weight on balls of feet ___
4. Draw arms back and to sides ___
5. Focus on the ball ___

Execution

6. Dive forward to intercept flight of ball ___
7. Body parallel to ground ___
8. Tilt head back ___
9. Neck firm ___
10. Arms extended forward and downward ___
11. Eyes open and mouth closed ___
12. Contact ball on forehead ___

Follow-Through

13. Momentum forward through point of contact with ball ___
14. Break fall with arms ___
15. Jump to feet ___

HEADING SKILLS SUCCESS STOPPERS

For many players heading is the weakest part of their game. Correct execution of heading skills requires coordination of movement, precise timing of the jump, and the sheer determination to outjump opponents for the ball. Beginners often have difficulty combining all elements simultaneously. Here is a list of common heading errors and some suggestions for correcting them.

Error	Correction
Jump Header	
1. The ball does not travel in the desired direction.	1. You probably neglected to square your shoulders to the ball or failed to contact the ball on your forehead. The flat area of your forehead just above the eyebrows provides the best heading surface. Face the ball, square your shoulders, and keep your neck and head firmly positioned as you contact the ball.
2. You fail to contact the ball at the highest point of your jump.	2. Correct timing of the jump is probably the most difficult element of the heading technique. Most beginners tend to jump too late and are still moving upward as the ball arrives. Try to jump early, hang suspended in the air for a moment or two, and then snap your upper trunk and head forward to meet the oncoming ball.
3. The headed ball lacks power and velocity.	3. You probably failed to snap your upper body and head forward to impact the ball. It is essential that you attack the ball; don't let the ball attack you. While in the air, try to maintain the arched position until the last moment, then powerfully snap your upper trunk and head forward to contact the ball.
4. Heading the ball gives you a headache.	4. This may occur if you contact the ball on the top or side of your head or if you fail to keep your neck and head firmly positioned at the moment of impact with the ball. Contact the ball on the flat surface of your forehead, tuck your chin, and keep your neck firm.

Error	Correction
Dive Header	
1. Your header lacks power and accuracy.	1. You probably mistimed your dive or failed to keep your neck firm and head steady as you headed the ball. Tilt your head back, keep your neck firm, and contact the ball on the flat surface of your forehead.
2. The ball pops off your head and goes up in the air.	2. You probably contacted the ball too high on your forehead or dipped your head as the ball arrived. Keep your head and neck firmly positioned and contact the ball on the central area of your forehead.
3. You get the wind knocked out of you as you contact the ground after heading the ball.	3. You may be so intent on heading the ball that you forget to cushion your fall to the ground. Extend your arms forward and downward as you dive to head the ball. This arm movement not only provides added momentum to your dive but also enables you to cushion your fall with your hands and arms.

HEADING SKILLS

DRILLS

1. Jump and Head Stationary Ball

Stand facing a teammate approximately 3 feet away. The teammate holds a ball above and to the front of his or her head. Take a step forward, jump straight up, and snap forward from the waist to contact the ball on your forehead. Combine all elements of the jump-header technique. Repeat 30 times, then switch roles with your teammate.

Success Goal = 25 of 30 balls contacted on forehead ___

✔ *Success Check*

• Jump straight up ___
• Arch upper body ___
• Tuck chin ___
• Eyes open and mouth closed ___

To Increase Difficulty

• Increase number of repetitions.
• Increase the speed of repetition.
• Require teammate to hold the ball higher.

To Decrease Difficulty

• Reduce number of repetitions.
• Teammate holds ball at head height so you don't have to jump.

2. Jump Header to Partner

Stand facing a teammate 5 yards away. He or she tosses a ball to a point approximately 12 to 18 inches above your head. Use a two-footed takeoff to jump up and head the ball back to your teammate. Contact the ball on your forehead at the highest point of the jump. Execute 20 headers, then switch roles with your partner.

Success Goal = 17 of 20 tosses headed directly to teammate's chest ___

Success Check
• Two-footed takeoff ___
• Arch upper trunk ___
• Eyes open and mouth closed ___
• Snap forward at waist ___

To Increase Difficulty
• Move farther from server.
• Execute headers at maximum speed.
• Increase number of repetitions.

To Decrease Difficulty
• Move closer to server.
• Slow the speed of repetition.

3. Jump Header Competition

This drill is similar to the preceding one except that a second server adds extra pressure. Use markers to outline a 5-by-10-yard area. Position a server at each end of the area while you position in the center. Servers alternate tossing a ball toward you. Move to the ball, jump up and head it back to the server who tossed it, and then turn to head a ball tossed by the opposite server. Alternate heading tosses from one server and then the other. Award one point for each ball headed to a server so that he or she can catch it directly out of the air. Execute 30 jump headers, then switch places with one of the servers and repeat. Each player should take two turns in the center for a total of 60 balls headed.

Success Goal = Score 50 or more points ___

Success Check
• Square shoulders to target ___
• Two-footed takeoff ___
• Snap upper trunk forward ___
• Contact ball on forehead ___

To Increase Difficulty
• Increase heading distance.
• Increase speed of repetition.
• Increase number of repetitions.

To Decrease Difficulty
• Execute header without jumping.
• Decrease number of repetitions.
• Execute headers at half speed.

4. Heading Races—Front to Back

Play with a group of teammates divided into equal-size teams. Position teams side by side in single file with 3 yards distance between teams. One player from each team positions as a server 3 yards in front of the first player in his or her line. The server has a ball and faces his or her teammates. On signal each server tosses a ball to the first player in his or her line who heads it back to the server and then drops to his or her knees. Servers immediately toss to the next player in line who also heads and then kneels. Servers continue through the line until reaching the last player at which point all team members have headed and are kneeling. After the last player in line heads to the server, the next to the last in line stands to receive a toss and head it to the server. The race continues, from back to front, until all players are again standing and the server has control of the ball. The team whose server goes through the entire line of players, front to back to front, in the least time wins the race. Repeat with a different team member as server. The first team to win five races wins the competition.

Success Goal = Win 5 races ___

Success Check
- Arch upper body back ___
- Neck stiff and chin tucked ___
- Snap forward from waist ___
- Contact ball on forehead ___

To Increase Difficulty
- Increase heading distance.
- Add players to each team.

To Decrease Difficulty
- Reduce heading distance.
- Reduce players per team.

5. Toss, Head, and Catch

Form a triangle with two teammates with about 10 yards distance between players. Designate yourself as Player 1 and your teammates as Players 2 and 3. Begin by tossing a ball to Player 2 who jumps and heads the ball to Player 3. Player 3 catches the ball and tosses it to you. Jump up and head the ball to Player 2 who catches and tosses it to Player 3. Continue the throw-head-catch routine until each player has executed 30 jump headers. Try to head the ball directly to your teammate so that it does not bounce to the ground.

Success Goal = 25 of 30 tosses headed directly to teammate ___

Success Check
- Two-footed takeoff ___
- Square shoulders to target ___
- Contact ball on forehead ___
- Eyes open and mouth closed ___

To Increase Difficulty
- Increase distance between players.
- Perform drill while slowly jogging around the field.

To Decrease Difficulty
- Reduce distance between players.
- Head without jumping.
- Slow the speed of repetition.

6. Moving Headers

Station on a touchline of the field facing a partner (server) who is standing 5 yards onto the field with a ball. The server begins to jog slowly backward and while doing so tosses a lofted ball toward you. Move forward, jump up to meet the ball, and head it back to your partner so he or she can catch the ball directly out of the air. Continue jogging across the field as you head tosses from the server. When you get to the opposite sideline, reverse direction and return to your starting point. Try to maintain the 5-yard distance from the server at all times. Head 25 tosses, then switch roles with the server and repeat.

Success Goal = 20 of 25 tosses headed to server's chest ___

Success Check
- Use two-footed takeoff to jump ___
- Arch upper body ___
- Eyes open and mouth closed ___
- Contact ball on forehead ___

To Increase Difficulty
- Increase heading distance.
- Increase jogging speed.
- Increase number of repetitions.

To Decrease Difficulty
- Decrease heading distance.
- Walk instead of jog.
- Don't jump when heading ball.

7. Heading to Score

Play with two teammates. Use markers to outline a 10-by-12-yard area. Place two cones to represent a goal 4 yards wide on one end of the area. Station one teammate as the goalkeeper, one to the side of the goal as a server, and you position 10 yards front and center of the goal as the "header." The server tosses the ball up so that it will drop near the center of the area. Judge the flight of the ball, move forward, and attempt to score by heading past the goalkeeper. Award two points for a goal scored, one point for a ball headed on goal but saved by the goalkeeper. Players rotate positions after each header. Continue until each player has performed 30 headers.

Success Goal = Score 35 or more points ___

Success Check
- Use two-footed takeoff ___
- Jump straight up ___
- Arch upper trunk ___
- Contact ball on forehead ___

To Increase Difficulty
- Reduce size of goal.
- Increase number of repetitions.

To Decrease Difficulty
- Head ball from standing position (without jumping).
- Increase goal width to 6 yards.

8. Heading Goal to Goal

Use markers to outline a rectangular area 10 by 15 yards. Position cones or flags to represent a goal 4 yards wide at each end of the area. You position in one goal with a ball; a teammate positions in the opposite goal. Toss the ball so that it will drop near the center of the area. Your teammate moves forward and attempts to score by heading the ball past you through your goal. Award two points for a goal scored and one point for a ball headed on goal but saved. Alternate turns trying to score off headers. Return to your respective goal after each attempt. Use either the jump- or dive-header technique. Perform 30 headers each. The player scoring the most points wins the game.

Success Goal = Score the most points ___

Success Check
- Square shoulders to ball ___
- Jump straight up ___
- Contact ball on forehead ___
- Head ball downward toward goal line ___

To Increase Difficulty
- Reduce goal width to 3 yards.
- Increase heading distance.

To Decrease Difficulty
- Execute headers without jumping.
- Increase goal width to 6 yards.
- Reduce heading distance.

9. Dive Header to Partner

Practice this drill in a sawdust pit, on a gymnastic mat, or on soft ground. Face a server who is standing approximately 10 yards away. The server tosses a ball parallel to the ground at approximately waist height toward you. Step toward the ball, dive forward parallel to the ground, and head the ball back to the server using proper dive-header technique. Head the ball so that the server does not have to move more than one step in any direction to catch it. Extend your arms downward to cushion your fall. After each header, immediately jump up and prepare to head again. Head 10 tosses in succession, then switch positions with the server.

Success Goal = 7 of 10 tosses headed directly to the server ___

Success Check
- Dive parallel to ground ___
- Tilt head back ___
- Neck stiff ___
- Eyes open and mouth closed ___
- Contact ball on forehead ___

To Increase Difficulty
- Increase number of repetitions.
- Perform dive header while jogging around field.

To Decrease Difficulty
- Start on all fours when heading the ball.
- Move closer to server.
- Decrease the repetitions.

10. Score off Dive Headers

Divide into two teams of four players each. Position teams side by side in single file about 15 yards from a regulation goal. Station a neutral goalkeeper in the goal. Position a server 5 yards to each side of the goal. Servers take turns tossing a ball into the area front and center of the goal. Players from both teams alternately attempt to score off dive headers. The goalkeeper tries to save all shots. Award 2 points for each goal scored and 1 point for a ball headed on goal but saved by the goalkeeper. The first team to score 50 points wins.

 **Success Goal** = Score 50 team points ___

 **Success Check**
• Dive parallel to ground ___
• Tilt head back with neck stiff ___
• Contact ball on forehead ___
• Extend arms to cushion fall ___

To Increase Difficulty
• Decrease goal size.

To Decrease Difficulty
• Move players closer to goal.
• Play without a goalkeeper.

11. Score by Headers Only (With Neutrals)

Organize into two teams of three players each with two additional neutral players who always play on the team with the ball. Use markers to outline a 25-by-35-yard playing area. Designate a goal 4 yards wide at the center of each endline. Award one team possession of the ball to begin. Do not use goalkeepers.

Passing is accomplished by throwing and catching, not kicking, the ball. Goals are scored by heading a ball tossed by a teammate through the opponent's goal. Players may take a maximum of five steps with the ball before passing to a teammate. Violation of the five-step rule results in loss of possession to opponents. The two neutrals always play with the attacking team to create a five-to-three-player advantage. Although there are no goalkeepers, all players may intercept passes or block shots with their hands. The defending team gains possession of the ball after an opponent's score, when it intercepts a pass, when an opponent drops the ball to the ground, or when the ball is played out of bounds and last touched by an opponent. Defending players may not wrestle the ball from an opponent. Play for 15 minutes. The team scoring the most goals wins the game.

Success Goal = Score the most goals ___

Success Check
• Square shoulders to goal ___
• Contact ball on forehead ___
• Head ball down to goal line ___

To Increase Difficulty
• Decrease goal size.
• Play with goalkeepers.
• Play with only one neutral.

To Decrease Difficulty
• Increase goal size.
• Play with three neutrals.

SUCCESS SUMMARY

It is essential that you develop the ability to play in the air as well as on the ground. Focus on these key points when practicing heading skills.

• When executing a jump header try to contact the ball at the highest point of your jump. Hold the arched position until the last possible moment, then snap forward into the ball. Keep your head and neck firmly positioned.

• When executing a dive header be sure to extend your body parallel to the ground as you dive forward to meet the ball. Tilt your head back, keep your neck firm, and contact the ball on your forehead.

Because it is sometimes difficult to visualize whether you are heading the ball correctly, it is a good idea to have a coach or teammate observe you practice the different heading techniques. The observer can evaluate your performance and, if necessary, offer helpful feedback.

The most widely recognized players throughout the soccer world are the goal scorers. Pele, who scored more than 1,200 goals as a professional, is without question the most popular player of all time. Today, almost 20 years after the end of Pele's career, soccer players everywhere still know his name, and his popularity continues to soar. During the 1994 World Cup it was the goal scorers, players such as Romario of Brazil and Jurgen Klinsmann of Germany, who attracted the most fan and media attention. Although scoring a goal is most often the result of a team effort, the player who puts the finishing touch on a successful attack receives much of the acclaim, and rightly so.

Your success as a goal scorer depends on several factors. The ability to shoot powerfully and accurately with either foot is essential. Qualities such as anticipation, determination, and composure under pressure are also important. A bit of luck doesn't hurt either, but as the saying goes, "Good luck is where preparation meets opportunity." Prepare to take advantage of scoring opportunities by practicing shooting skills in situations that simulate actual game conditions. Learn to vary your shots depending on whether the ball is rolling, bouncing, or dropping from the air. Basic shooting skills include the *instep drive, full volley, half volley, side volley,* and *swerving,* or bending, shots.

Why is Shooting Important?

The final objective of every attack is to score a goal. Easier said than done, however! In the real world you will fail to achieve your objective more often than not because scoring goals is, quite simply, the most difficult task in soccer. To score goals on a regular

basis you must be able to execute shooting skills under the game pressures of limited time, restricted space, physical fatigue, and aggressive opponents.

How to Execute the Instep Drive Shot

Use the instep drive to strike a rolling or stationary ball. The kicking mechanics are very similar to those used for the instep pass except that there is greater follow-through motion of the kicking leg. Approach the ball from behind and at a slight angle. Plant your balance foot beside the ball with the knee of your balance leg slightly flexed. Keep your head steady and focus on the ball. Draw your kicking leg back and extend your kicking foot. At this point the knee of your kicking leg should be directly over the ball. Snap your leg straight and contact the center of the ball with the full instep of your foot. Your foot must be firm and pointed down as it strikes the ball. Square your shoulders and hips to the target. Use a complete follow-through motion to generate maximum power on the shot (see Figure 5.1).

How to Execute Volley Shots

Most players find volley shots more difficult to execute than the instep drive. This is not surprising because it requires precise timing as well as correct technique to strike a ball out of the air. Even so, some of the most spectacular goals I've seen have been scored off volleys. Master these shooting skills, and you will be well on your way to becoming a dangerous goal scorer.

FIGURE
5.1 **KEYS TO SUCCESS**

INSTEP DRIVE SHOT

Preparation

1. Approach the ball from behind and at slight angle ___
2. Plant balance foot beside ball ___
3. Flex balance leg at knee ___
4. Arms out to sides for balance ___
5. Draw back kicking leg ___
6. Extend kicking foot ___
7. Head steady ___
8. Focus on the ball ___

Execution

1. Square shoulders and hips with target ___
2. Body over ball ___
3. Snap kicking leg straight ___
4. Keep kicking foot firm ___
5. Contact center of ball with instep ___

Follow-Through

1. Momentum forward through point of contact ___
2. Complete follow-through motion of kicking leg ___
3. Balance foot lifts off ground ___

Full Volley Shot

Use the full volley to shoot a ball directly out of the air. Move to the spot where the ball will drop. Flex your nonkicking leg at the knee for improved balance and body control. Draw your kicking leg back and extend your kicking foot. Keep your head steady and always watch the ball. Snap your kicking leg straight and contact the center of the ball with the full instep. Square your shoulders and hips to the target. Your kicking foot must be firm and pointed down at the moment of contact with the ball. This stance positions the knee of your kicking leg above the ball. Proper foot and knee position is required to keep the shot low. Use a short, powerful kicking motion as the leg snaps straight (see Figure 5.2).

FIGURE
5.2

KEYS TO SUCCESS

FULL VOLLEY SHOT

Preparation

1. Move to spot where ball will drop ___
2. Face the ball with your shoulders square ___
3. Flex balance leg at knee ___
4. Draw back kicking leg ___
5. Extend kicking foot ___
6. Arms out to sides for balance ___
7. Head steady ___
8. Focus on the ball ___

Execution

1. Square shoulders and hips to target ___
2. Knee of kicking leg over ball ___
3. Snap kicking leg forward from knee ___
4. Kicking foot firm ___
5. Contact center of ball with instep ___

Follow-Through

1. Kicking leg snaps straight ___
2. Momentum forward ___

Half Volley Shot

The half volley is similar in many respects to the full volley. The primary difference is that the ball is volleyed at the instant it contacts the ground rather than directly out of the air. Anticipate where the ball will drop and move to that spot. Draw your kicking leg back and fully extend your kicking foot. Square your shoulders and hips to the target. Snap your kicking leg straight and contact the center of the ball with your instep at the moment the ball hits the ground. Use a short, powerful kicking motion rather than a complete follow-through (see Figure 5.3).

FIGURE 5.3

HALF VOLLEY SHOT

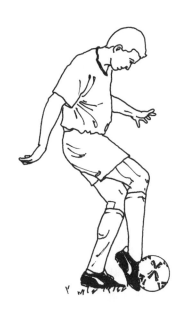

Preparation

1. Move to spot where ball will drop ___
2. Face the ball with shoulders square ___
3. Flex balance leg ___
4. Draw back kicking leg ___
5. Extend and firmly position kicking foot ___
6. Arms out to sides for balance ___
7. Head steady ___
8. Focus on the ball ___

Execution

1. Square shoulders and hips to target ___
2. Knee of kicking leg over ball ___
3. Snap kicking leg from knee ___
4. Point kicking foot down and keep it firm ___
5. Contact center of ball as it hits ground ___

Follow-Through

1. Snap kicking leg straight ___
2. Momentum forward ___

Side Volley Shot

Use the side volley to shoot a ball that is bouncing or dropping to your side. Most players find this shooting technique the most difficult to execute successfully. In preparation to shoot turn your body sideways so that your front shoulder is pointing in the direction that you want the ball to travel. Raise your kicking leg to the side so it is almost parallel to the ground. Draw back your kicking foot by flexing your leg at the knee. Keep your head steady and focus on the ball. Snap your kicking leg straight and contact the top half of the ball with your instep. Keep your foot firm and fully extended. The follow-through motion of your kicking leg should travel on a slightly downward plane (see Figure 5.4).

FIGURE
5.4

KEYS TO SUCCESS

SIDE VOLLEY SHOT

Preparation

1. Position body sideways ___
2. Raise kicking leg to side parallel to ground ___
3. Draw back kicking leg; flex at knee ___
4. Extend kicking foot ___
5. Weight on balance leg ___
6. Flex balance leg ___
7. Arms out to sides for balance ___
8. Head steady ___
9. Focus on the ball ___

Execution

1. Rotate half turn toward ball on balance foot ___
2. Snap kicking leg from knee ___
3. Contact top half of ball with instep ___
4. Point front shoulder toward target ___

Follow-Through

1. Snap kicking leg straight ___
2. Angle kicking motion slightly downward ___
3. Drop kicking foot to ground ___

How to Execute a Swerving Shot

Sometimes the most direct path to goal may not be the best route. Shots that curve in flight are difficult to catch and may fool opposing goalkeepers. You can cause your shot to swerve by imparting spin to the ball. Begin your approach from a position almost directly behind the ball. Plant your balance foot beside the ball with head steady and eyes focused on the ball. Draw back your kicking leg and extend your kicking foot. Snap your leg straight and contact the ball with the inside or outside portion of your instep. If you use your right foot and contact the outer half of the ball with the inside portion of your instep, the shot will curve inward. Use an outside-in follow-through motion of the kicking leg. If you contact the inside half of the ball with the outside of your instep, the shot will curve outward. Use an inside-out follow-through motion of the kicking leg. Keep your kicking foot firmly positioned as it contacts the ball. Use a complete follow-through motion to generate greater power and swerve (see Figure 5.5).

FIGURE 5.5 **KEYS TO SUCCESS**

SWERVING SHOT

Preparation

1. Approach ball from directly behind ___
2. Plant balance foot beside ball ___
3. Flex balance leg at knee ___
4. Draw back kicking leg ___
5. Extend kicking foot ___
6. Arms out to sides for balance ___
7. Head steady ___
8. Focus on the ball ___

Execution

1. Momentum forward ___
2. Contact ball left or right of its vertical midline with inside or outside of instep ___
3. Keep kicking foot firm ___

Follow-Through

1. Drive foot through point of contact with ball ___
2. Use inside-out kicking motion for outside-of-instep shot ___
3. Use outside-in kicking motion for inside-of-instep shot ___
4. Follow-through motion to waist level or higher ___

SHOOTING SKILLS SUCCESS STOPPERS

Your three main objectives when executing the various shooting techniques are accuracy, power, and low trajectory of the shot. If you consistently fail to achieve one or more of these objectives you probably won't score many goals. Common shooting errors are listed here along with suggestions for correcting them.

Error	Correction
Instep Drive, Full Volley, and Half Volley Shots	
1. Your shot travels over the goal.	1. You probably positioned your balance (nonkicking) foot behind the ball, which caused you to lean back as you kicked it. Instead, plant your balance foot beside the ball. Your kicking foot should be fully extended and pointed down as it contacts the ball. This will ensure that your body is over the ball. Snap your kicking leg straight and continue your momentum forward through the point of contact with the ball.
2. Your shot lacks power.	2. A weak shot is usually due to insufficient follow-through motion of the kicking leg or failure to transfer weight forward as your foot contacts the ball. When executing the instep drive, the follow-through motion of your kicking leg should continue upward to approximately chest height. A complete follow-through motion is not necessary for volley shots, but your kicking leg should snap straight as your foot contacts the ball.
3. Your shot pulls wide of the goal.	3. Square your shoulders and hips to the goal as you kick the ball. Keep your head steady and foot firm as you strike the ball with the full surface of your instep. Use a complete follow-through motion.
4. You fail to contact the ball on your instep.	4. This error usually occurs when you take your eye off the ball or, with the half volley, when you mistime the kick.

Error	Correction
Side Volley Shot	
1. Your shot lacks power.	1. This occurs because you swing your kicking leg into the ball rather than snap the lower half of your leg into the ball. Keep your leg in the cocked position until the last possible moment; then snap it straight and drive your foot through the center of the ball with a short, powerful motion.
2. Your shot travels up and over the goal.	2. This occurs because you failed to get your leg above the ball and as a result contacted the lower half of the ball. The knee of your kicking leg should be even with or above the ball at the moment you kick it. Your kicking motion should travel on a downward plane through the top half of the ball.
Swerving Shot	
1. Your shot fails to curve in flight.	1. You did not impart sufficient spin on the ball. Contact the ball left or right of its vertical midline, not directly through its center. Use an inside-out kicking motion for the outside-of-the-instep shot and an outside-in kicking motion for the inside-of-the-instep shot.
2. Your shot lacks power.	2. A weak shot is usually due to one or more of the following errors: (a) Your foot makes contact too close to the ball's outer edge, (b) your foot is not firmly positioned as it contacts the ball, or (c) you have insufficient follow-through motion. Keep your kicking foot firm and contact the ball just right or left of its center. Try to get as much of your instep on the ball as possible. You need a complete follow-through motion to generate enough power and spin to swerve the ball's flight path.

SHOOTING SKILLS

DRILLS

1. Shooting From Set Pieces

Use masking tape or chalk to outline a regulation-size goal on a wall or kickboard. Use the instep-drive technique to shoot a stationary ball (set piece) on goal from a distance of approximately 20 yards. Collect each rebound, reposition the ball at a different spot, and shoot again. Take 20 shots with each foot. Award yourself one point for each shot on goal.

Success Goal = 32 of 40 points ___

Success Check
- Square shoulders and hips to goal ___
- Knee over ball ___
- Kicking foot extended and firm ___
- Head steady with vision on ball ___
- Complete follow-through ___

To Increase Difficulty
- Shoot from 25 yards.
- Make goal smaller.
- Execute swerving shots.

To Decrease Difficulty
- Shoot from 15 yards.
- Make goal larger.

2. Shoot to a Partner

Have a teammate roll a ball to you from 10 yards away. Shoot the rolling ball back at your teammate using the instep-drive technique. Take 20 shots with each foot, then switch roles with your teammate. Award yourself one point for each shot kicked so that your teammate can catch the ball without moving more than one step to either side.

Success Goal = 30 of 40 points ___

Success Check
- Square shoulders and hips to target ___
- Knee over ball ___
- Kicking foot extended and firm ___
- Head steady ___

To Increase Difficulty
- Move 15 yards from partner.
- Increase velocity of serve.
- Take all shots with weakest foot.
- Execute full volley shots on balls tossed from server.
- Execute half volley shots on balls tossed from server.

To Decrease Difficulty
- Move 5 yards from partner.
- Take all shots with favorite (strongest) foot.
- Shoot stationary ball to partner.

3. Score Through the Central Goal

Place two cones 8 yards apart to represent a regulation-size goal. Position yourself with a ball 25 yards from the goal. A teammate positions 50 yards away from you on the opposite side of the goal. Dribble forward 3 or 4 yards and attempt to shoot the ball through the goal. Your teammate retrieves the ball and attempts to score in the same manner. Award yourself one point for each shot that travels between the cones below head height. Shoot back and forth with your teammate until you have each taken 40 shots—20 with each foot. All shots must be taken from a distance of at least 20 yards.

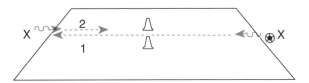

 **Success Goal** = 30 of 40 possible points ___

✔ **Success Check**
• Square shoulders and hips to goal ___
• Kicking foot extended and firm ___
• Complete follow-through ___

To Increase Difficulty
• Increase shooting distance to 25 yards.
• Make goal smaller.
• Require swerving shots.

To Decrease Difficulty
• Decrease shooting distance to 15 yards.
• Make goal larger.

4. First-Time Shooting Competition

Play with two teammates at one end of a regulation field. One teammate positions as the goalkeeper. You position 30 yards from the goal with a supply of balls. The third player positions as a "target" 20 yards from goal. Pass a ball to the target who pushes it about a yard to either side. Sprint forward and shoot the ball first time (without controlling it) using the instep-drive technique from a distance of approximately 20 yards. The goalkeeper tries to save all shots. Follow your shot to score off a rebound if the goalkeeper fails to hold the ball. Players rotate positions after each shot and repeat the exercise. Award one point for a shot on goal saved by the goalkeeper and two points for a goal scored. Play until each player completes 30 first-time shots.

Success Goal = 40 of 60 possible points ___

✔ **Success Check**
• Square shoulders and hips to goal ___
• Knee over ball ___
• Kicking foot extended and firm ___
• Head steady and focus on the ball ___
• Complete follow-through ___

To Increase Difficulty
• Increase shooting distance to 25 yards.
• Reduce goal width to 6 yards.
• Require shooter to volley first-time shots.

To Decrease Difficulty
• Reduce shooting distance to 15 yards.
• Allow two-touch shooting.
• Use cones to represent an enlarged goal.

5. Toss and Volley to Goal

Position with a supply of balls 20 yards front and center of a regulation goal. A teammate positions as the goalkeeper. Toss a ball upward into the air so it drops a couple of yards in front of you. Move to the ball, allow it to bounce once, and then full volley the ball on goal. Repeat with half volley and side volley shots. Take 10 shots with each type of volley (5 with each foot) for a total of 30 volleys, then switch places with the goalkeeper. Award yourself one point for a shot on goal, two points for a goal scored.

 **Success Goal** =

14 or more points with full volley ___
12 or more points with half volley ___
10 or more points with side volley ___

Success Check

• Square shoulders and hips to goal ___
• Knee over ball ___
• Head steady ___
• Kicking leg snaps straight ___

 To Increase Difficulty

• Increase shooting distance.
• Decrease goal size.
• Volley a ball tossed by server.

To Decrease Difficulty

• Reduce shooting distance.
• Increase goal size.
• Volley the ball directly out of your hands.

6. Two-Touch Shooting to Score

Position yourself 25 yards front and center of a regulation goal. Position a server on the flank area with a supply of balls. The server crosses balls into the penalty area for you to control and shoot on goal. Try to control each crossed ball with your first touch, then shoot to score with your second touch. Perform 30 repetitions using the shooting technique of your choice. Award yourself one point for each crossed ball that you control and shoot into the goal using only two touches. Do not use a goalkeeper.

Success Goal = 20 or more points ___

Success Check

• Prepare ball with first touch ___
• Kicking foot extended and firm ___
• Square shoulders and hips to goal ___
• Head steady and watch the ball ___
• Complete follow-through ___

 To Increase Difficulty

• Increase shooting distance.
• Add a passive defender to the drill.
• Shoot first time without controlling the ball.

To Decrease Difficulty

• Reduce shooting distance.
• Allow shooter three touches to control and shoot the ball.

7. Pressure Shooting in the Penalty Area

Play on one end of a regulation field. Position a goalkeeper in goal and a server 25 yards from goal with 10 soccer balls. You stand directly in front of the server with your back to the goal. The server rolls a ball past you into the penalty area. Quickly turn and sprint to the ball, shoot to score, and then sprint back to your original spot. The server immediately rolls a second ball past you. Again you turn, sprint to the ball, and shoot to score. You must shoot each ball first time, without stopping or controlling it. The server alternates rolling balls to your left and right feet. Take 10 shots, then switch positions with the server and repeat the round. Award two points for each goal scored and one point for each shot on goal saved by the goalkeeper. Play three rounds as the shooter and three as the server.

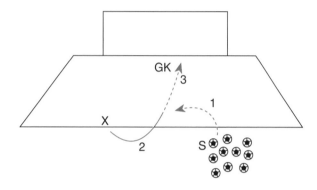

Success Goal = 12 or more points per round ___

Success Check
• Square shoulders and hips to goal ___
• Kicking foot extended and firm ___
• Head steady ___
• Snap leg straight ___
• Complete follow-through ___

To Increase Difficulty
• Increase shooting distance.
• Take 15 shots per round.
• Shoot bouncing balls.

To Decrease Difficulty
• Reduce shooting distance.
• Decrease speed of repetition.
• Allow shooter two touches to control and shoot the ball.

8. Game With a Central Goal

Play with four teammates in an area of approximately 30 by 30 yards. Position two cones or flags in the center of the area to form a goal 8 yards wide. Designate one teammate as the neutral goalkeeper and organize the remaining players into teams of two players each. The goalkeeper positions between the goalposts and attempts to save all shots. Your team begins with possession of the ball; the opponents must defend. Score goals by kicking the ball through either side of the central goal below the height of the goalkeeper. The goalkeeper must readjust his or her position depending on the location of the ball. A ball that goes out of play is returned by throw-in. If the defending team gains possession of the ball, it immediately switches to the attack and tries to score. After making a save, the goalkeeper tosses the ball to a corner of the playing area where both teams compete for possession. Play nonstop for 20 minutes and keep track of the score.

Success Goal = Score the most goals ___

Success Check
- Shoot at every opportunity ___
- Square shoulders and hips to goal ___
- Head steady and watch the ball ___

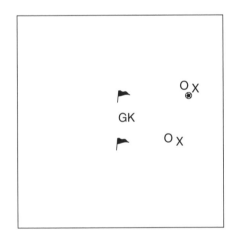

To Increase Difficulty
- Reduce goal size.
- Limit players to three or fewer touches to pass or shoot the ball.
- Add one neutral player who always plays on the defending team to create a one-player advantage for the defending team.

To Decrease Difficulty
- Enlarge the goal.
- Add one neutral player who always plays with the team in possession to create one-player advantage for the attacking team.

9. Goal Scoring Derby

Play with five teammates on one end of a regulation soccer field. Designate one teammate as the goalkeeper, one as the server, and divide the remaining players into two teams. Both teams position themselves in the 18-by-44-yard penalty area. The goalkeeper positions in the common goal, and the server positions at the top of the penalty area with 10 to 12 soccer balls. To begin the drill the server tosses a ball into the penalty area. Both teams vie for possession; the team that wins the ball attempts to score while the other team defends. If a defending player steals the ball, his or her team immediately attacks and tries to score. The goalkeeper is neutral and attempts to save all shots. Immediately after a goal is scored, or the keeper makes a save, or the ball is kicked out of the penalty area, the server tosses another ball into play. Continue the exercise until all the soccer balls are used. The team scoring the most goals wins the competition. Reorganize the teams, designate a new goalkeeper and a new server, and repeat the drill.

 **Success Goal** = Score the most goals ___

✔ **Success Check**
- Quick release of shot ___
- Kicking foot extended and firm ___
- Square shoulders and hips to goal ___

 To Increase Difficulty
- Use cones or flags to represent a smaller goal.
- Add one player who always plays with the defending team creating an advantage for the defense.

To Decrease Difficulty
- Use cones or flags to represent an enlarged goal.
- Add one player who always plays on the team with the ball creating an advantage for the attackers.

10. Long-Distance Shooting Game

Divide into two teams of four players each. Use cones or flags to outline a 35-by-60-yard field area with a regulation-size goal at the center of each endline. One player on each team plays as a goalkeeper. Each team defends a goal and tries to score in the opponent's goal. Begin with a kickoff from the center of the field. Regular soccer rules apply except that all shots must be taken from a distance of 15 yards or greater. Award two points for a goal scored and one point for a shot on goal saved by the goalkeeper. Play for 20 minutes. Rotate a different player into the goal every 5 minutes so that each player takes a turn as goalkeeper.

Success Goal = Score the most points ___

✔ **Success Check**
- Square shoulders and hips to target ___
- Kicking foot extended and firm ___
- Knee over ball ___
- Complete follow-through ___

 To Increase Difficulty
- Require shots to be taken from at least 20 yards.
- Decrease goal width to 6 yards.
- Require first-time shots.
- Require that goals be scored off volley shots.

To Decrease Difficulty
- Allow scores from any distance.
- Increase goal width to 10 yards.
- Do not use goalkeepers.

SUCCESS SUMMARY

Developing your ability to shoot with power and accuracy is the first step toward becoming a proficient goal scorer. Ask your coach or a teammate to observe and analyze your shooting technique during practice sessions. The observer should focus his or her attention on the position of your balance foot and kicking foot, the position of your hips and shoulders in relation to the goal, the position of the knee of your kicking leg in relation to the ball, and your follow-through motion. The observer should identify your major shortcomings and provide corrective feedback.

Once you are able to execute the various shooting skills successfully in a low-pressure, practice-type situation, you should refine your skills in situations that include the game pressures of restricted time and space, physical fatigue, and tough challenges from opponents. Use the drills described in Step 5 to achieve these objectives.

STEP 6

GOALKEEPING: THE LAST LINE OF DEFENSE

The goalkeeper is arguably the most important player on the soccer team. He or she provides the last line of defense for the team and must master a set of skills entirely different from those used by the field players. The goalkeeper is the only player allowed to use the hands to receive and control the ball and can do so only within the team's own penalty area. To play as a goalkeeper you must be able to catch or block all types of shots directed at your goal. At times you will have to dive through the air to save shots to either side. You may even have to deny an opponent on a breakaway—and making the save is only half the job! You are also responsible for initiating your team's attack by distributing the ball accurately to teammates. The goalkeeper position is a demanding one, both physically and mentally, and it requires a special type of athlete.

Goalkeeping skills include the basic stance, commonly referred to as the *ready position*; methods of receiving low, medium, chest-high, and high balls; methods of diving; and methods of distributing the ball by rolling, throwing, dropkicking, or punting. Although a team usually designates one or two players specifically as goalkeepers, all players should understand goalkeeping skills. Young players (under 12 years of age) should not specialize in the goalkeeper position but instead should split time between the playing in the goal and in the field.

Why Are Goalkeeping Skills Important?

The goalkeeper is the one true specialist on the soccer team. Assigned the task of protecting a goal 8 feet high and 24 feet wide, he or she poses the final obstacle that opponents must bypass to score. A good goalkeeper is competent in a variety of specialized goalkeeping skills.

The Goalkeeper Stance

Assume the basic goalkeeper stance, that is, the ready position, when an opponent has the ball within shooting distance of your goal. From the ready position you will be able to move quickly in any direction. Square your shoulders to the ball with feet approximately shoulder-width apart. Keep your head and upper body erect and knees slightly flexed. Center your body weight forward over the balls of your feet so that your heels raise slightly off the ground. Position your hips and buttocks as if you were sitting on a medium-height stool. Carry your hands at approximately waist level with palms forward and fingers pointing upward. Keep your head steady and focus on the ball (see Figure 6.1).

How to Receive Ground Balls

Making the routine play on a regular basis is just as important as making the occasional spectacular play. In fact, the majority of your saves will probably be of the routine variety unless your teammates decide not to play any defense in front of you. Most of the saves you will make involve ground, or rolling, balls. You will use three different techniques to receive ground balls depending on the nature of the shot.

Ball Rolling Directly at Goalkeeper

Use the technique commonly referred to as the *standing save*. From the ready position quickly shuffle sideways to a position between the ball and the goal. Keep your legs straight with feet a few inches apart and bend forward at the waist as the ball arrives. Extend your arms downward with palms forward and slightly cupped. Your forearms should be almost parallel with one another, and your fingertips should almost touch the ground. Do not try to catch the ball on your palms. Allow the ball to roll up onto your wrists and forearms, then return to an upright position with the ball clutched securely against your chest (see Figure 6.2).

Low Driven Shot Directly at Goalkeeper

The conventional standing save is not appropriate for a low, powerfully driven shot aimed directly at the goalkeeper or for a shot that skips just in front of the goalkeeper. This is especially true when playing on a wet field surface where the ball accelerates upon hitting standing water or wet grass. To compensate for the added velocity of such shots, the goalkeeper should use a receiving technique commonly referred to as the *forward vault*. From the ready position bend forward at the waist, flex your knees, and vault forward and down to the ground at the oncoming ball. Extend your arms and hands underneath the ball with palms facing up. The ball should actually contact your wrists and forearms, not your hands. As the ball arrives fall forward on your forearms and trap it between your chest and forearms. Your legs should be extended behind you and slightly spread for balance (see Figure 6.3).

Ball Rolling to the Side of Goalkeeper

In some instances you won't have time to position yourself to make the standing save. This type of shot,

Figure 6.1 The ready position: feet approximately shoulder-width apart, weight balanced and centered over balls of feet, head and upper body erect.

sometimes called the *tweener*, is just far enough away to make the standing save impossible but not so far as to require a diving save. To make the save, move laterally across the goal to intercept the rolling ball. Extend your lead foot in the direction you are moving and flex your leg at the knee. Kneel on the trailing leg and align it parallel to the goal line. Allow only a small space between the heel of your lead foot and the knee of the trailing leg to prevent the ball from skidding through your legs. From this position bend your upper body forward with shoulders square to the ball. Allow the ball to roll up onto your wrists and forearms before clutching it to your chest (see Figure 6.4).

FIGURE 6.2 **KEYS TO SUCCESS**

BALL ROLLING DIRECTLY AT GOALKEEPER

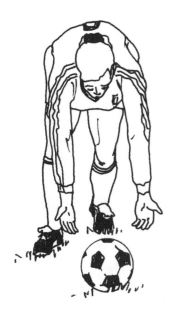

Preparation

1. Assume ready position ___
2. Position between ball and goal ___
3. Erect posture ___
4. Feet a few inches apart ___
5. Focus on the ball ___

Execution

1. Bend forward at waist ___
2. Legs straight ___
3. Arms extended downward ___
4. Palms forward and cupped ___
5. Contact ball on palms ___
6. Allow ball to roll onto wrists and forearms ___

Follow-Through

1. Withdraw body slightly upon impact ___
2. Return to standing position ___
3. Clutch ball against chest with forearms ___
4. Distribute the ball ___

**FIGURE
6.3**   **KEYS TO SUCCESS**

LOW DRIVEN SHOT
DIRECTLY AT GOALKEEPER

Preparation

1. Assume ready position ___
2. Position body between ball and goal ___
3. Focus on the ball ___

Execution

1. Bend forward at waist ___
2. Flex knees ___
3. Shoulders square to ball ___
4. Vault forward to ground ___
5. Arms extended with palms facing up ___
6. Ball contacts wrists and forearms ___

Follow-Through

1. Fall forward onto fore-arms ___
2. Trap ball between forearms and chest ___
3. Legs extended behind and slightly spread ___
4. Jump to feet ___
5. Distribute the ball ___

FIGURE
6.4 **KEYS TO SUCCESS**

BALL ROLLING
TO THE SIDE OF GOALKEEPER

Preparation

1. Assume ready position ___
2. Shuffle laterally across goal ___
3. Extend lead foot and flex knee ___
4. Kneel on trailing leg ___
5. Align trailing leg parallel to goal line ___
6. Focus on the ball ___

Execution

1. Bend forward at waist ___
2. Shoulders square to ball ___
3. Head steady ___
4. Palms forward and fingers extended ___
5. Let ball roll onto wrists and forearms ___

Follow-Through

1. Clutch ball to chest with forearms ___
2. Hop to feet ___
3. Distribute the ball ___

RECEIVING GROUND BALLS SUCCESS STOPPERS

Most errors that occur when receiving ground balls are due to improper positioning of the body and legs. It is important that you move into position as quickly as possible and prepare to receive the ball in advance of its arrival.

Error	Correction
1. You attempt to make a standing save, but the ball rolls through your hands, between your legs, and into the goal.	1. Position your body behind the ball with your feet only a few inches apart. If the ball happens to slip between your hands, it will rebound off your legs rather than roll into the goal.
2. When you make a standing or kneeling save, the ball rebounds off your hands into the area in front of the goal.	2. This error may occur if you try to catch rather than scoop the ball. Remember, you do not catch a rolling ball with your hands. Allow the ball to roll up onto your wrists and forearms, then use a scooplike motion of your arms as you return to an upright position and clutch the ball to your chest.
3. When you use the forward-vault technique, the ball slips between your arms and underneath you into the goal.	3. You failed to position your forearms close together beneath the ball as you received it. Vault forward to meet the ball; keep your arms extended and parallel to one another. Keep your forearms a few inches apart. As the ball arrives, scoop it up and clutch it between your chest and forearms.

How to Receive Air Balls

The goalkeeper must also be able to receive and hold balls that arrive through the air. Powerful shots from outside the penalty area and balls crossed or served into the goal area from the flanks pose a challenge for the goalkeeper. How you receive the ball will depend upon the height and flight path of the shot.

Medium-Height Balls

A medium-height ball is one that arrives between your ankles and waist. To receive a ball arriving at ankle height, use a scoop technique similar to that used when receiving a ball rolling directly at you. Position your body behind the ball with legs straight and feet a few inches apart. As the ball arrives, bend forward at the waist. Extend your arms downward with palms facing forward. Receive the ball on your wrists and forearms, then secure it against your chest. Do not attempt to catch the medium-height ball in the palms of your hands.

To receive a ball arriving at waist height, bend forward at the waist with forearms parallel to one another and extended down. Receive the ball on your forearms. As it arrives, jump backward a few inches to absorb its impact. The harder the shot, the more cushion you must provide to keep the ball from bouncing away from you (see Figure 6.5).

Chest-High or Head-High Balls

Square your shoulders with the oncoming ball. Hold your hands at approximately chest height with palms facing forward and fingers spread and extended toward the oncoming ball. As the ball arrives, position your hands in what is generally referred to as the *W (window) position*, with fingers spread and thumbs almost touching. Extend your arms toward the ball with slight flexion at the elbow. In contrast to the

FIGURE
6.5

KEYS TO SUCCESS

RECEIVING A MEDIUM-HEIGHT BALL

Preparation

1. Position yourself in line with the ball ___
2. Upright posture with legs a few inches apart ___
3. Arms extended downward ___
4. Fingers pointed down and palms forward ___
5. Focus on the ball ___

Execution

1. Bend forward at the waist ___
2. Knees slightly flexed ___
3. Forearms parallel to one another ___
4. Contact ball on wrists and forearms ___

Follow-Through

1. Jump a few inches backward to cushion shot ___
2. Allow ball to roll up onto forearms ___
3. Clutch ball with forearms against chest ___
4. Distribute the ball ___

scoop technique used to receive low shots, you should catch a chest-high ball on your fingertips. Withdraw your arms to cushion the impact and secure the ball to your chest.

Follow the hands-eyes-head (HEH) principle of goalkeeping when receiving a chest-high or head-high ball. Position your hands, eyes, and head in line with the ball as you receive it. Follow the flight of the ball into your hands by looking through the window formed by your thumbs and index fingers (see Figure 6.6).

High-Lofted Balls

Receiving and controlling high-lofted balls may be your most difficult test. Success requires correct technique, balance and body control, precise timing, and good judgment. Face the ball as it approaches the goal area; keep shoulders square. Move toward the ball and use the *one-leg takeoff* to generate maximum upward momentum. The jumping technique looks quite similar to that used when shooting a lay-up in basketball. Try to catch the ball at the highest point possible by extending your arms overhead.

FIGURE 6.6

KEYS TO SUCCESS

RECEIVING A CHEST-HIGH OR HEAD-HIGH BALL

Preparation

1. Position between ball and goal ___
2. Square shoulders ___
3. Feet shoulder-width apart ___
4. Hands at chest level ___
5. Palms forward ___
6. Fingers extended toward ball ___
7. Head steady and watch the ball ___

Execution

1. Extend arms toward ball with hands in W position ___
2. Elbows slightly flexed ___
3. Look through "window" ___
4. Receive ball on fingertips ___

Follow-Through

1. Withdraw hands and arms ___
2. Secure ball to chest ___
3. Distribute the ball ___

You must leap off the correct foot. When receiving a ball crossed from the flank, thrust your outside leg (toward the field) upward with knee flexed. Point the knee toward the ball to ensure that your shoulders are square to the ball. The leg closest to the goal remains straight and serves as the balance leg. Thrust your arms and leg upward in one fluid movement to generate the greatest momentum. Position your hands in the W position and follow the HEH principle. Watch the ball until the moment it contacts your hands, then secure it to your chest. Drop to the ground on your balance leg (see Figure 6.7).

FIGURE
6.7

**FIGURE
6.7**

KEYS TO SUCCESS

RECEIVING A HIGH-LOFTED BALL

Preparation

1. Face the oncoming ball ___
2. Shoulders square ___
3. Move toward the ball ___
4. Head steady and focus on the ball ___

Execution

1. Use one-leg takeoff to jump ___
2. Arms and outside leg (toward field) thrust upward in one fluid motion ___
3. Inside (balance) leg remains straight ___
4. Arms extended up with hands in W position ___
5. Head behind hands (HEH) ___
6. Receive ball at highest point of jump ___
7. Receive ball on fingers and palms ___

Follow-Through

1. Withdraw arms and hands ___
2. Descend to ground ___
3. Land on balance leg ___
4. Secure ball to chest ___
5. Distribute the ball ___

RECEIVING AIR BALLS SUCCESS STOPPERS

Errors that occur when receiving balls out of the air are usually due to improper positioning of the hands or body, poor timing of the jump, or both. Common errors are listed here along with suggestions for correcting them.

Error	Correction
Receiving a Medium-Height Ball	
1. You fail to hold the ball.	1. Receive the ball on your wrists and forearms, then clutch it to your chest. Do not attempt to catch the ball in your hands.
2. The ball rebounds off your arms and out of your control.	2. Jump back a few inches as the ball arrives to absorb its impact.
Receiving a Chest-High or Head-High Ball	
1. The ball slips through your hands.	1. Position your hands close together to form a window (the W position). Thumbs and forefingers should almost touch behind the ball as you receive it.
2. The ball bounces off your hands and out of your control.	2. Receive the ball on your fingertips, not on the palms. Flex your elbows and withdraw your arms as the ball arrives to soften its impact.
Receiving a High-Lofted Ball	
1. You fail to catch the ball at the highest possible point.	1. Thrust your arms and takeoff leg upward in one fluid motion to generate maximum height on your jump.
2. The ball goes over your head and into the goal.	2. Face the ball and judge its flight path. Move toward the oncoming ball in preparation to jump. Wait until the last possible moment, then use a one-leg takeoff to leap upward and receive the ball at the highest point of your jump.

How to Dive to Save Shots

The sight of a goalkeeper diving fully extended to save a shot is one of the most exciting and acrobatic moments in soccer. The initial diving movement begins from the ready position with vision focused on the ball. You must coordinate the movement of your legs and upper body to vault toward the spot where you can intercept the ball. Take a step with the foot nearest the ball in the direction you are going to dive. Push off that foot to begin your dive; for example, push off your right foot when diving to your right. Your opposite leg and arm follow to generate additional momentum. Extend your arms and hands toward the ball. When possible, use the HEH principle to ensure correct positioning of your body behind the ball. Position your hands in a sideways version of the W position and receive the ball on your fingertips and palms. Place your lower hand behind the ball with elbow tucked to your side. Your upper hand comes down hard on top of the ball, pinning it to the ground. After making the save, contact the ground on your side, not on your stomach. Landing on your stomach increases the chance of injury because the position exposes your back to an overly aggressive opponent (see Figure 6.8).

If you are unsure of catching and holding the ball, follow this basic rule of goalkeeping: When in doubt, parry it out. You can parry, or deflect, the ball wide of the goal with the open palm of your lower hand. Angle your hand slightly back and keep the wrist firm. Contact the inside half of the ball with your open palm to deflect the ball wide of the goal.

How to Distribute the Ball

After making the save, you must initiate your team's attack by quickly rolling, throwing, or kicking the ball to a teammate.

Distribute the Ball by Rolling

Rolling, or bowling, the ball is an effective means of distributing the ball over distances 20 yards or less. The motion looks similar to that used when bowling. Cup the ball in the palm of your hand, step toward the target, and release the ball with a bowling-type motion. Release the ball at ground level to prevent bouncing (see Figure 6.9).

Distribute the Ball by Throwing

You can distribute the ball over longer distances by throwing or kicking it. Throwing has two advantages over kicking: greater accuracy and quicker delivery. Goalkeepers use two popular throwing techniques. Use the *baseball throw* to toss the ball over medium distances of 20 to 35 yards. Release the ball with a motion similar to that used when throwing a baseball. Hold the ball in the palm of your hand, step toward the target, and use a three-quarter or overhand throwing motion. Snap your wrist toward the target to add velocity to the throw (see Figure 6.10).

Use the *javelin throw* to toss the ball over longer distances. Curl your hand around the ball, encasing it with your fingers, palm, and wrist. Extend your throwing arm back and keep it straight. Arch your body backward. At this point you should be holding the ball behind you at approximately waist level. Step toward the target and snap your upper body forward from the waist. The throwing motion of your arm moves along an upward arc and ends with a whip-like motion of the arm above your head. You can release the ball at any point along the throwing arc, depending upon the type of trajectory you desire. The sooner you release the ball along the throwing arc, the higher the trajectory. The ball will travel almost parallel to the ground if you release it near the completion of your throwing motion (see Figure 6.10).

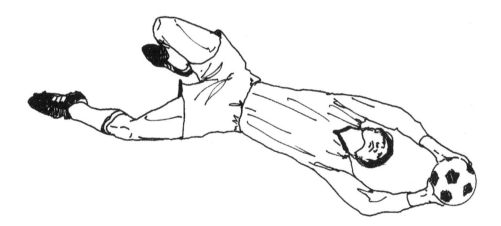

Figure 6.8 Extend arms and hands toward ball, eyes on the ball; contact ground on your side.

FIGURE 6.9 **KEYS TO SUCCESS**

DISTRIBUTION BY ROLLING

Preparation

1. Face your target ___
2. Cup ball in palm of hand ___
3. Step toward target with leg opposite the throwing arm ___

Execution

1. Bend forward at waist ___
2. Draw back arm and ball ___
3. Release ball at ground level with bowling-type motion ___
4. Head steady and focus on the target ___

Follow-Through

1. Follow-through motion with throwing arm ___
2. Resume erect posture ___

FIGURE
6.10

KEYS TO SUCCESS

DISTRIBUTION BY THROWING

Baseball Throw

Preparation

1. Face the target ___
2. Hold ball in palm of hand ___
3. Cock arm behind ear ___
4. Head steady and focus on the target ___

Execution

5. Step toward target with foot opposite throwing arm ___
6. Use three-quarter or overhand throwing motion ___
7. Snap wrist toward target ___
8. Release ball ___

Follow-Through

9. Complete follow-through of throwing arm ___

Javelin Throw

Preparation

1. Encase ball in fingers, palm, and wrist ___
2. Extend throwing arm back with body sideways to target ___
3. Extend opposite arm toward target ___
4. Arch upper body backward ___
5. Hold ball at waist level ___
6. Head steady and focus on the target ___

Execution

7. Step toward target ___
8. Whiplike motion of throwing arm along upward arc ___
9. Release ball ___

Follow-Through

10. Complete follow-through of throwing arm ___

Distribute the Ball by Kicking

Although less accurate than throwing, kicking is an excellent means of quickly sending the ball into the opponent's end of the field. The two most common kicking techniques are the full volley punt and dropkick.

To execute a *full volley punt* stand erect and face your target. Hold the ball in the palm of the hand opposite your kicking foot and extend that arm forward so the ball is approximately waist level. Keep your head steady and watch the ball. Step forward with the nonkicking foot, release the ball, and then volley the ball out of the air using a complete follow-through motion of the kicking leg. Square your shoulders and hips to the target and contact the center of the ball with the instep surface of your kicking foot. Your foot should be fully extended and firmly positioned (see Figure 6.11).

The *dropkick*, or half volley, can be used as an alternative to the full volley. The kicking mechanics are nearly identical except that, rather than the ball being volleyed directly out of the air, foot contact occurs just as the ball impacts the ground. Lean back slightly and keep your kicking foot firmly positioned as it strikes the ball. Square your shoulders and hips to the target and use a complete follow-through motion. The dropkick is a good choice on windy days because the flight path of the ball is generally lower than a full volley punt. If the field surface is wet or bumpy, however, the full volley punt is a better option (see Figure 6.12).

Figure 6.12 Release ball, step forward, and strike ball with instep at the instant ball contacts ground. Lean back and use complete follow-through motion of kicking leg.

Figure 6.11 Step forward with the nonkicking foot, release ball, contact ball on instep of kicking foot. Use complete follow-through motion.

BALL DISTRIBUTION SUCCESS STOPPERS

Accuracy is more important than distance when it comes to distribution. It doesn't matter how far you can throw or kick the ball if it usually goes to a player on the other team. You can improve performance on both counts—distance and accuracy—by devoting a portion of practice time to developing your throwing and kicking skills. Common errors that occur when distributing the ball are listed here along with suggested corrections.

Error	Correction
Rolling the Ball	
1. The ball bounces toward the target.	1. You released the ball above ground level. A smooth release at ground level will result in a ball that rolls smoothly along the ground.
Throwing the Ball	
1. Your throw lacks accuracy.	1. Step toward the target and use a complete follow-through motion. When using the baseball throw, snap your wrist toward the target as you release the ball. When using the javelin throw, point your nonthrowing arm toward the target as you prepare to throw the ball.
2. Your throw lacks distance.	2. When executing the baseball throw, step toward the target and use a complete follow-through motion of the throwing arm. When using the javelin throw, fully extend your throwing arm behind you; then use a whiplike motion of the arm along an upward arc to propel the ball toward the target.
Kicking the Ball	
1. Your punt or dropkick lacks accuracy.	1. Step toward the target with your nonkicking foot. Square your shoulders and hips to the target. Contact the center of the ball with the full instep surface of your kicking foot.
2. Your punt or dropkick lacks distance.	2. Lack of distance is usually due to insufficient follow-through of the kicking leg. Keep your foot firmly positioned and kick through the point of contact with the ball. Your kicking foot should swing upward to waist level or higher.

DRILLS

1. Handling

Hold a ball with both hands at approximately chest level. Bounce the ball hard off the ground and receive it with the W catch before it rises above your waist. Repeat 40 times.

Success Goal = 36 of 40 bounces caught and held ___

Success Check
- Hands in W position ___
- Catch ball on fingertips ___
- Withdraw hands to cushion impact ___

To Increase Difficulty
- Bounce ball very hard off the ground and catch it before it travels above your thighs.
- Bounce and catch while walking or jogging.

To Decrease Difficulty
- Bounce ball more softly off the ground.

2. Toss and Catch

Stand facing a teammate 6 yards away. Toss a ball to the right or left of your teammate's chest or head. He or she must receive the ball using the W catch and the HEH principle. Your teammate then tosses the ball to you to receive in the same manner. Attempt to catch 40 tosses each.

Success Goal = 38 of 40 tosses caught and held ___

Success Check
- Head steady ___
- Focus on the ball ___
- Hands, eyes, and head aligned with ball ___
- Hands in W position ___
- Receive ball on fingertips ___

To Increase Difficulty
- Increase velocity of tosses.
- Put spin on tosses.
- Perform drill while shuffling sideways.
- Catch volleys from teammate.

To Decrease Difficulty

- Move closer to teammate.
- Toss ball very softly.

3. Standing Save

Play with two teammates who act as servers. The servers, each with a ball, face one another 12 yards apart while you position midway between them. Servers alternate turns rolling a ball to you. Receive each ball using the standing-save technique, return it to the server, then immediately turn to receive a rolling ball from the opposite server. Receive 30 balls using the standing-save technique, then switch places with one of the servers and repeat the drill. Award one point for each ball received and held without rebound.

Success Goal = 28 of 30 possible points ___

✔ Success Check
- Bend forward at waist with legs together and straight ___
- Allow ball to roll onto wrists and forearms ___
- Scoop ball to chest ___
- Return to standing position ___

To Increase Difficulty
- Increase velocity of serves.
- Increase speed of repetition.
- Increase number of repetitions.

To Decrease Difficulty
- Serve slowly rolling balls.
- Decrease number of repetitions.

4. Post to Post (Footwork)

Three servers, each with a ball, position themselves an equal distance apart along the 6-yard line in front of a regulation goal. You position next to one of the goalposts facing the servers. Server 1 (directly in front of you) rolls a ball that you receive and return. Shuffle across the goal mouth as Server 2 tosses a medium-height ball at you. Receive the ball, return it to Server 2, and continue to shuffle sideways. When you reach the opposite post, Server 3 tosses you a chest-high or head-high ball, which you also receive and return. Continue shuffling back and forth from post to post until you have received 30 balls.

Success Goal = 26 of 30 balls received and held ___

✔ Success Check
- Do not cross legs when shuffling ___
- Position body behind the ball ___

To Increase Difficulty
- Increase speed of side-shuffle movement.
- Increase velocity of serves.

To Decrease Difficulty
- Side shuffle at a walking pace.
- Do not vary the type of service (i.e., rolling balls only).

5. Saving the Tweener Ball

Play in a regulation goal. Select two teammates to act as servers. You position as goalkeeper near the right goalpost and face the servers. Position a server in line with each goal post, 10 yards out from the goal line. Server 1 (directly in front of you) rolls a ball to your left, toward the center of the goal. Move to your left, receive the ball using the kneeling-save technique, and return the ball to Server 2. Continue moving sideways across the goal mouth. When you reach the left post, Server 2 rolls the ball to your right, toward the center of the goal. Move laterally to the ball, receive it using the kneeling save, and return the ball to Server 1. Continue shuffling back and forth from post to post until you have received 20 rolling balls.

Success Goal = 18 to 20 balls received without error ___

Success Check
- Extend lead foot toward ball ___
- Kneel on trailing leg ___
- Align trailing leg parallel to goal line ___
- Leave only a few inches between lead heel and trailing knee ___
- Allow ball to roll up onto wrists and forearms ___
- Clutch ball to your chest ___

To Increase Difficulty
- Increase velocity of serves.
- Increase speed of repetition.
- Increase number of repetitions.

To Decrease Difficulty
- Decrease speed of repetition.
- Decrease number of repetitions.

6. Forward-Vault Save

Kneel facing a partner 5 yards away who is also kneeling. Toss a ball that bounces or skips directly in front of your partner. He or she must fall forward, with palms facing up and forearms underneath the ball, to receive the ball. Your partner returns the ball in a similar manner for you to receive using the forward-vault technique. Continue until each of you has executed 20 forward-vault saves. Award one point for each shot held without a rebound.

Success Goal = Score 15 or more points ___

Success Check
- Fall forward from knees ___
- Scoop the ball with palms up and forearms underneath the ball ___
- Forearms parallel to each other ___
- Clutch ball to chest ___

To Increase Difficulty
- Increase velocity of throws.
- Vary trajectory of throws.
- Forward vault from a squat position.
- Forward vault from standing position.

To Decrease Difficulty
- Reduce velocity of throws.

7. Diving From Knees

Assume a kneeling position with a ball placed to each side within your reach. Practice falling to your left, then right, then left, and so on to pin the stationary ball to the ground. Emphasize the correct technique of landing on your side while placing one hand behind ball and one on top to pin it to ground. Repeat 10 times to each side.

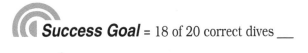**Success Goal** = 18 of 20 correct dives ___

✔ **Success Check**
• Fall sideways ___
• Tuck elbow of lower arm to side ___
• Land on side and hip ___
• Pin ball to ground with one hand on top and one behind ___

To Increase Difficulty
• Move balls slightly farther apart.
• Increase number of repetitions.
• Increase speed of repetition.
• Move balls farther from you and dive from a squat position.

To Decrease Difficulty
• Decrease the number of repetitions.

8. Standing Dive

Assume the ready position and face a teammate standing 8 yards away. The teammate serves a rolling ball 3 to 4 yards to your side. Dive to save the shot, then return the ball to the server. Attempt 10 saves to each side. As a variation the server can toss balls at waist height.

Success Goal = 7 of 10 balls saved to each side ___

✔ **Success Check**
• Step sideways with foot nearest ball ___
• Vault toward spot of save ___
• Extend arms and hands toward ball ___
• Contact ground on side ___
• Pin ball to ground ___

To Increase Difficulty
• Increase velocity of serves.
• Increase speed of repetition.
• Increase number of repetitions.
• Dive over a greater distance to save.

To Decrease Difficulty
• Move closer to the server.
• Decrease velocity of serves.

9. Receiving the High Ball

While jogging, toss a ball high in the air. Use a one-leg takeoff to jump up and catch the ball at the highest point of your jump. Toss and receive 30 high balls. Alternate right- and left-leg takeoffs.

Success Goal = Catch 25 or more tosses at highest point of jump ___

Success Check
- Thrust arms and takeoff leg upward in one smooth motion ___
- Position hands in the W position ___
- Catch ball at highest point of jump ___

To Increase Difficulty
- Increase height of toss.
- Compete with a teammate when jumping to catch the ball.

To Decrease Difficulty
- Walk rather than jog.
- Don't leave ground when receiving ball.
- Decrease number of repetitions.

10. High-Ball Training

Three servers are positioned in a circle around you at a distance of approximately 12 yards. Each server in turn tosses a high-lofted ball toward the center of the circle. Square your shoulders to the descending ball, leap up using the correct takeoff leg, and catch the ball at the highest possible point of your jump. Receive 30 tosses. Alternate using left and right leg as takeoff leg.

Success Goal = 25 of 30 tosses received at highest point of jump ___

Success Check
- Use one-leg takeoff to jump ___
- Point knee of takeoff leg toward ball ___
- Extend arms and hands above head ___
- Hands in W position ___

To Increase Difficulty
- Increase the number of repetitions.
- Position two keepers who compete for the high ball in the center of the circle.

11. Distribute by Throwing

Distribute the ball by throwing it to a partner over varying distances. Select the method of distribution depending upon the distance to be covered:

- Rolling balls—15 yards
- Baseball throw—30 yards
- Javelin throw—45 or more yards

A throw is "accurate" if your partner does not have to move more than three steps in any direction to receive the ball. Perform 20 repetitions of each type of throw.

Success Goal =

18 of 20 accurate rolling balls ___
15 of 20 accurate baseball throws ___
12 of 20 accurate javelin throws ___

Success Check

- Step toward target ___
- Use complete follow-through motion ___
- Distribute ball to partner's feet ___

To Increase Difficulty

- Increase distance from partner.
- Define an accurate throw as one that drops within two steps of partner.

To Decrease Difficulty

- Reduce throwing distance.
- Define an accurate throw as one that drops within six steps of the receiver.

12. Distribute by Kicking

Position with a supply of balls near one penalty spot of a regulation field. Use markers to outline a 15-yard-square target area in the opposite half of the field just past the midline. Attempt to punt (volley) or half volley the ball so that it lands within the target area. Award yourself two points for each ball that drops within the square on the fly and one point for each ball that bounces into and through the target area. Execute 20 volley punts and 20 half volleys.

Success Goal =

25 or more points with full volley punt ___
25 or more points with half volley ___

Success Check

- Square shoulders with target ___
- Extend arms and hold ball at approximately waist height ___
- Keep head steady and focus on ball ___
- Contact the ball through its center ___
- Complete follow-through motion of kicking leg ___

To Increase Difficulty

- Decrease size of target area.
- Increase distance to target area.

To Decrease Difficulty

- Increase size of target area.
- Decrease distance to target area.

SUCCESS SUMMARY

To master the skills needed to become a top-flight netminder requires a great deal of time and effort. Begin by walking through each technique; gradually increase the speed of repetition as you feel more confident and comfortable with the movements. Eventually progress to more challenging, game-simulated practice situations. Ask your coach or a fellow goalkeeper to observe you execute the receiving (shot-saving) and distribution skills discussed in this chapter. He or she can evaluate your performance and provide helpful feedback.

If you are really serious about becoming a top goalkeeper, you should read *The Soccer Goalkeeper* (2nd edition) published by Human Kinetics. The book provides an in-depth analysis of the skills and tactics used by the #1 player on the soccer field.

STEP 7

GROUP ATTACK: CREATING NUMBERS-UP SITUATIONS

Although each player must be able to execute the individual skills and tactics discussed thus far, the team will not experience success as a whole unless all players channel their collective efforts toward a common goal. Much like the pieces of a puzzle, individual players must fit together in the correct combinations to complete the picture. If they do, team performance can exceed the sum total of individual talents. This is the ultimate goal of all team sports, that the so-called whole (team) be greater than the sum of its parts (players). On the other hand, if teammates cannot or will not work in combination with one another, then team play will suffer no matter how talented the individual players.

Two important attacking tactics are the *give and go pass* and *support*. The give and go pass is an effective tactic to penetrate a packed defense and also to bypass an opponent on your way toward the opponent's goal. Support in attack refers to the movement of attacking players in the vicinity of the ball. With proper support the attacking team can create the passing combinations it needs to maintain possession of the ball and score goals.

Why Are Group Tactics in Attack Important?

Outstanding individual play sometimes results in spectacular goals. During the 1994 World Cup, players such as Romario of Brazil and Roberto Baggio (1993 FIFA Player of the Year) of Italy demonstrated their ability to almost single-handedly determine the outcome of a match with sudden bursts of brilliance on the field. In most cases, however, successful at-

tacking play is the result of the coordinated efforts of two or more teammates. One important key to attacking success is to get more attacking players than defending players in the vicinity of the ball. This is commonly referred to as a *numbers-up situation*.

How to Execute the Give and Go Pass

The most fundamental numbers-up situation is the two-versus-one situation, that is, two attackers versus one defender. The primary tactic used to beat a defender in a two-versus-one situation is the give and go, or wall, pass.

The concept of give and go is simple. The player with the ball (first attacker) dribbles at and commits the defending player to him or her, then passes the ball to a nearby teammate (second attacker) before sprinting into the space behind the defender to collect a return pass. (You *commit* the defender when he or she steps forward to tackle the ball.)

Sounds easy, but successful execution of the give and go pass is rather complex. First of all, the defender is trying to prevent it! In addition, both the player with the ball and his or her teammate must fulfill specific responsibilities in order for the give and go pass to work. Precise skill execution, correct timing of pass and run, and a conceptual understanding of the basic tactics are all essential for success.

When you are the *first attacker* in a two-versus-one situation, it is your responsibility to initiate the action. Perform the following steps in the order listed.

1. *Take on the defender.* Immediately dribble at (take on) the defending player as soon as you recognize that a numbers-up situation exists. Your action

will force the defender to make an immediate decision—either to retreat and delay your forward movement or to challenge for possession of the ball.

2. *Commit the defender.* Draw the defending player to you.

3. *Pass the ball.* Release your pass as the defender closes to tackle. Use the outside surface of your instep to pass the ball to the lead foot of your teammate.

4. *Sprint forward into space.* Sprint into the space behind the defending player after you pass the ball.

5. *Collect the return pass.* Receive a one-touch pass from your teammate.

When you are the *second attacker* in a two-versus-one situation, you must perform the following steps.

1. *Move to a position near the ball.* Recognize the opportunity for a give and go pass. Position yourself 3 to 4 yards to the side of the defending player at an angle of approximately 45 degrees from the first attacker.

2. *Position as "the wall."* Use an open stance with your body turned toward the first attacker. Your lead foot will serve as the wall off which he or she will pass the ball.

3. *Execute a one-touch pass into space.* Redirect the pass from the first attacker into the space behind the defender.

4. *Support your pass.* Sprint forward to support your teammate after passing the ball. Another give and go situation could develop immediately (see Figure 7.1).

<table>
<tr><td>FIGURE
7.1</td><td>**KEYS TO SUCCESS**</td></tr>
</table>

GIVE AND GO PASS

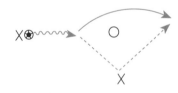
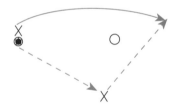

Player With Ball (First Attacker)

Preparation

1. Face the defender ___
2. Head up and watch the field ___

Execution

3. Dribble at defender ___
4. Commit defender to you ___
5. Release pass using outside-of-the-foot technique ___
6. Pass to lead foot of support player ___

Follow-Through

7. Sprint forward into space behind defender ___
8. Receive one-touch (wall) pass behind defender ___
9. Advance toward goal ___

Support Player (Second Attacker)

Preparation

1. Move to position near the ball ___
2. Position 3 to 4 yards to side of defending player ___
3. Use open stance and watch the ball ___
4. Maintain open passing lane to first attacker ___

Execution

5. Extend lead foot ___
6. Position foot at proper angle ___
7. Keep foot firm ___
8. Contact ball on inside of foot ___
9. Redirect pass into space behind defender ___

Follow-Through

10. Sprint forward ___
11. Look for another give and go opportunity ___

How to Execute Support in Attack

It is essential that the first attacker have several passing options. This is accomplished through a tactic commonly referred to as *support in attack*. Proper support enables your team to consistently create numbers-up situations in the vicinity of the ball. A lack of support leaves the player with the ball isolated from teammates and increases the chances that he or she will lose possession.

Providing adequate support for the first attacker depends on several factors, including the (a) number of support players, (b) angle of support, and (c) distance of support.

Number of Support Players

The number of support players near the ball is of critical importance. Too few players (i.e., a lack of support) limits the first attacker's options. Too many attacking players near the ball can also be a disadvantage because they will draw additional defending players to the area. As the space around the ball becomes crowded with players, it becomes more difficult for the attacking team to execute passing combinations and maintain possession. As a general guideline, three teammates should support the player with the ball. A support player should be positioned to each side and slightly ahead of the ball. A third support player should be positioned behind the player with the ball.

Angle of Support

Support players should position themselves to form a wide angle with the first attacker. Imagine two lines drawn from the ball, one to each support player, that form a 90-degree or greater angle (see Figure 7.2). A defending player challenging for the ball cannot possibly cover two support players who are positioned at a wide angle of support, but may be able to do so if they are positioned at a narrow angle of support.

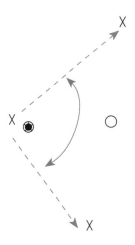

Figure 7.2 Support players should position at a wide angle of support from the ball so defender cannot cover both support players.

Distance of Support

How near should you position to the ball when providing support for a teammate? Base your decision on the following criteria: the position of defending player(s) and the area of the field. As a general rule, position yourself within 3 to 5 yards of the ball if the space is limited and a defending player is preparing to challenge for possession. You can support from a greater distance, possibly 8 to 10 yards, if a defending player is not preparing to challenge for possession or if the space around the ball is not crowded with players.

Reduce the distance of support when the ball is in the opponent's end of the field. Closer, more compact support is beneficial there because the defending team will usually position players to protect the dangerous scoring zone front and center of their goal. Close support in the opponent's end of the field opens up the possibility of using the give and go pass to beat a packed defense. The distance of support can be extended as the ball moves farther from the defending team's goal.

GROUP-ATTACK TACTICS SUCCESS STOPPERS

Tactical errors occur for a variety of reasons because both skill execution and decision making are involved in every situation. A poorly paced or inaccurate pass, improper position of the support player(s), failure of the dribbler to commit the defender, or release of the pass too soon or too late can all result in a breakdown of group-attack tactics. Common errors are listed here along with suggested corrections.

Error	Correction
Give and Go Pass	
1. You fail to commit the defender before passing to supporting teammate.	1. Dribble directly at the defender. As he or she steps forward to tackle the ball, execute the give and go pass with a supporting teammate.
2. You pass the ball to a supporting teammate but he or she cannot execute the give and go pass with you.	2. This can occur for two reasons. First, the support player may be positioned too far from you. Proper support position is 3 to 4 yards to the side of the defender; support at a greater distance gives the defender time to readjust his or her position to intercept the wall pass. Second, the give and go passing combination will also break down if you fail to sprint forward after passing the ball to the support player. Move forward into the space behind the defender immediately after releasing the pass.
3. You fail to recognize a numbers-up situation and do not attempt the give and go pass.	3. Keep your head up and watch the field. Numbers-up situations, particularly in the opponent's half of the field, won't last too long because additional defending players are trying to recover to positions goalside of the ball. It is essential that you be able to recognize a numbers-up situation immediately and take advantage of the opportunity to penetrate the opposing defense via a give and go pass.
Support in Attack	
1. An opponent blocks the passing lane between you and the ball.	1. Position yourself at a wide angle from the ball to create an open passing lane. Never position behind the defender or at a narrow angle where the defender can intercept the pass.
2. You fail to readjust your position in response to movement of the ball.	2. Support positioning should be in a state of constant flux. As the ball is played from one area of the field to another, players must readjust their positions to provide support in the area of the ball.

GROUP ATTACK

DRILLS

1. Playing the Wall

Execute the wall pass with a teammate against an imaginary defender as you jog the length of the field. Try to pass the ball to the lead foot of the wall who redirects the ball ahead into the space behind the imaginary defender. Award yourself one point for each pass to your teammate's lead foot. Award your teammate one point for each one-touch pass redirected forward into space behind the imaginary defender. Perform the drill at half speed. Execute 40 wall passes, then switch positions with the support player and repeat.

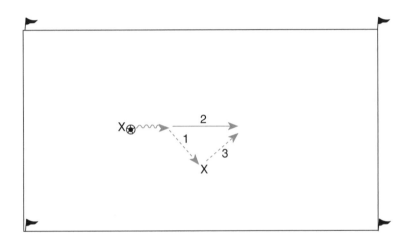

**Success Goal** =

35 of 40 possible points as the first attacker ___
35 of 40 possible points as the support player (wall) ___

Success Check

First Attacker:
• Dribble at imaginary defender ___
• Pass with outside surface of foot ___
• Sprint forward into space ___

Support Player:
• Position sideways to first attacker ___
• Redirect pass into space behind imaginary defender ___
• Move forward to support the ball ___

To Increase Difficulty
• Increase speed of execution.
• Add a defender to the drill.

To Decrease Difficulty
• Practice wall pass with stationary support player.

2. Two-Versus-One Possession Game

You and one teammate combine to play against a third player (defender) within a 12-by-12-yard grid. Use dribbling, shielding, and passing skills to maintain possession from the defender within the grid. Your team is allowed an unlimited number of touches to pass and receive the ball. Award two points each time your team executes a give and go pass to beat the defender and one point each time you and your teammate combine for five or more consecutive passes. Award the defender one point each time he or she intercepts a pass or forces your team to pass the ball outside of the grid area. Play for 5 minutes, then switch defenders and repeat.

Success Goal = Score more points than defender ___

Success Check
• Commit the defender ___
• Support player must maintain clear passing lane to the player with the ball ___

To Increase Difficulty
• Decrease grid size.
• Award attackers one point for seven consecutive passes.
• Limit attackers to three touches to pass and receive the ball.

To Decrease Difficulty
• Increase grid size.
• Award attackers one point for three consecutive passes.

3. Two-Versus-One to Line

Play with two teammates. Team with one player and position yourselves 25 yards from an endline of the field. The third player stands on the endline facing you with a ball. He or she serves the ball to you and immediately sprints forward to defend. Receive the ball and attempt to take on and beat the defender to the endline using a give and go pass with your teammate. Award your team one point if you beat the defender to the endline using the give and go pass. Repeat 10 times, then switch defenders and repeat.

Success Goal = 7 or more points scored ___

Success Check
• Take on and commit the defender ___
• Support player positions to side ___
• Pass to support player's lead foot ___
• Redirect pass into space behind defender ___

To Increase Difficulty
• Restrict attacking team to a 10-yard-wide zone when attempting to beat the defender.

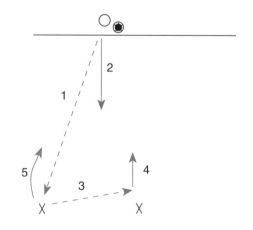

4. Two-Versus-One Plus One

Select three teammates to participate with you; organize into teams of two players each. Mark off a playing area of 20 by 30 yards with a goal 4 yards wide at the center of each endline. Each team defends a goal and tries to score in the opponent's goal. Your team begins the game with a kickoff from the center of the field.

The rules of play are as follows. The team in possession of the ball scores points by kicking it through the opponent's goal, by executing a successful give and go pass, or both. The defending team tries to prevent scores by positioning one player as a goalkeeper and one as a defender. Change of possession occurs when the defender steals the ball, the goalkeeper makes a save, the ball goes out of bounds last touched by a member of the attacking team, or a goal is scored.

When the original defending team gains possession of the ball, the goalkeeper immediately sprints out of the goal to join his or her teammate to attack the opponent's goal. The team losing possession must immediately defend: One player sprints back to play as the goalkeeper while his or her teammate positions as the defender. Once play begins, the action is continuous as teams attack with two players and defend with one player and a goalkeeper. Teammates alternate playing as the goalkeeper. Award one team point for each give and go pass that beats a defender and one additional point for each goal scored. Play for 15 minutes and keep track of points.

Success Goal = Score more points than opponent ___

Success Check
• Immediate transition from defense to attack ___
• Take on and commit defender ___

To Increase Difficulty
• Decrease goal size.
• Decrease width of field.
• Limit players to three or fewer touches.

To Decrease Difficulty
• Increase goal size.

5. Keep-Away Game (Three vs. One)

Designate one player as a defender and form a team of three attackers. Use markers to outline a 12-by-12-yard grid. The objective is for your team to keep the ball away from the defender within the boundaries of the grid. Attackers are free to move anywhere within the grid and are allowed unlimited touches to pass and receive the ball. Award one point for each time your team can make eight or more consecutive passes without losing possession. Play for 5 minutes, then switch defenders and repeat.

Success Goal = 4 or more points scored in 5 minutes ___

Success Check
• Immediate support of the ball ___
• Position at wide angles of support ___
• Correct pace and accuracy of passes ___

To Increase Difficulty
• Decrease size of grid.
• Limit attackers to two touches.
• Add a defender and play three versus two.

To Decrease Difficulty
• Increase size of grid.
• Add an attacker and play four versus one.

6. Four Corner Support Game

Play with seven teammates. Use markers to outline a 25-square-yard field area. Place a cone at the midpoint of each of the four sides with a support player stationed at each cone. Organize the remaining teammates and yourself into teams of two. You have the ball to begin.

You and your teammate try to maintain possession of the ball from your opponents within the grid. The four support players join the team with the ball to create a six-verses-two player advantage for the attack. Support players are restricted in their movement, however, and must remain within 1 yard on either side of their cone. Support players may receive the ball from and pass the ball to central players only; they may not pass among themselves. Change of possession occurs when a defending player steals the ball or when the ball goes out of play. Award one team point for six consecutive passes without possession loss. Play nonstop for 5 minutes, then central players switch positions with support players and repeat.

Success Goal = Score more points than opponents ___

Success Check
• Use give and go pass when possible ___
• Use support players as passing options ___

To Increase Difficulty
• Limit support players to one-touch passes.
• Award one team point for 10 consecutive passes.

To Decrease Difficulty
• Allow support players to move 3 yards from their cones.
• Allow support players to pass among themselves.

7. Short-Short-Long Possession Game

Select four teammates to participate with you. Use markers to outline a 35-by-40-yard area. You and two teammates form the attacking team. The remaining two players comprise the defending team. You have possession of the ball to begin.

The attacking team tries to keep the ball away from the defending team. Attackers are allowed an unlimited number of touches to pass and receive the ball. The only restriction on the attacking team is that every third pass must be 20 yards or greater in distance, a restriction that requires the attackers to constantly change the point of attack. *Short-short-long* refers to the required passing sequence. Award the attacking team two points for nine consecutive passes in the short-short-long sequence. Award the defending team one point each time it steals the ball or forces the attacking team to lose control of the ball outside of the area. If a defending player steals the ball, or the ball travels out of the area, immediately return the ball to the attacking team and resume play. Play for 5 minutes, then switch defenders and repeat.

Success Goal = Score more points than defenders ___

Success Check
• Provide close support for player with the ball ___
• Maintain wide angles of support ___
• Use entire field area to spread defenders apart and create passing lanes ___

To Increase Difficulty
• Limit attackers to three touches to pass and receive the ball.
• Add a defender and play three versus three.

To Decrease Difficulty
• Eliminate short-short-long passing requirement.
• Award three points for six consecutive passes.
• Add an attacker and play four versus two.

8. Split the Defense

Play with five teammates. Use markers to outline a rectangular area 12 by 20 yards. Designate two teammates as defenders and the remaining players and you as attackers. Attackers try to keep the ball away from the defenders by interpassing among themselves and attempt to *split*, or pass the ball between, defenders when possible. (This is commonly referred to as the *killer* pass, a pass that penetrates the defense.) If a defender steals the ball, or the ball leaves the playing area, the ball is quickly returned to an attacker and play resumes. Award the attacking team one point for six consecutive passes without loss of possession and two points for a completed pass that splits the defenders. Award defenders one point each time they steal the ball or force the attackers to play the ball out of the area. Play for 10 minutes, then designate two different players as defenders. Play three rounds with all players taking a turn as attackers.

Success Goal = Score more points than defenders ___

Success Check
• Position at wide angles of support ___
• Readjust position in response to movement of the ball ___
• Recognize opportunities for the killer pass ___

To Increase Difficulty
• Award one point for 10 consecutive passes.
• Limit attackers to two-touch passing.
• Reduce the size of the playing area.
• Add a defender and play four versus three.

To Decrease Difficulty
• Increase the size of the playing area.
• Add an attacker and play five versus two.

9. Small-Sided Game With Scoring Options

Play with two teams of five players each. Use markers to outline a 40-by-50-yard playing area with a 4-yard-wide goal positioned on the center of each endline. Each team defends a goal and can score in the opponent's goal. Do not use goalkeepers.

Begin with a kickoff from the center of the field. Regular soccer rules apply except that teams are awarded points for the following:

• One point for a successful give and go pass that beats an opposing player
• One point for six or more consecutive passes without possession loss
• Two points for a shot through the opponent's goal

Play for 25 minutes. The team scoring the most points wins the game.

Success Goal = Score more points than opponents ___

Success Check
• Recognize opportunities for the give and go pass ___
• Provide support for the player with the ball ___
• Maintain open passing lanes ___

To Increase Difficulty
• Decrease the size of the playing field.
• Limit players to three or fewer touches to pass and receive the ball.
• Use smaller goals.
• Use goalkeepers.

To Decrease Difficulty
• Enlarge the goals.
• Award one team point for four or more consecutive passes.

SUCCESS SUMMARY

Successful performance in group-attacking situations depends in large part on your ability to read the situation, choose the most appropriate action, and then implement that action through precise skill execution. In essence, you must correctly determine what to do, when to do it, and then be physically able to do it. Have your coach or a teammate observe you perform in a game. He or she should pay special attention to how you respond in specific situations. Do you usually choose the best course of action? If not, you must focus on improving your decisions. This should be a continuing process for all players. Even veteran professionals can sharpen their game through a more thorough understanding of group-attack tactics coupled with practice in game-simulated situations.

STEP 8

GROUP DEFENSE: PRESSURE, COVER, AND BALANCE

Defense and attack are really opposite sides of the same coin. Although each has different objectives, defense and attack are connected in the sense that players must be able to make quick and effective transitions from one to the other. *Pressure, cover,* and *balance* are the three most essential defensive tactics, and every player should understand the role of each tactic in the team's overall defensive scheme.

Why Are Pressure, Cover, and Balance Important?

Just as attacking players work in combination to create scoring opportunities for themselves, defending players use pressure, cover, and balance to prevent their opponents from scoring.

How to Execute Pressure, Cover, and Balance in Defense

The defender closest to the ball, generally referred to as the *first defender*, applies pressure at the point of attack. The job of the first defender is to prevent immediate penetration via the pass or dribble and to allow defending teammates time to recover to a position goalside of the ball.

Defensive cover ensures that one or more teammates support the first defender. The supporting teammate(s) is commonly referred to as the *second*, or covering, *defender*. The covering defender(s) positions to protect the space behind and to the side of the first defender. If the first defender is beaten on the dribble, the covering defender can step forward

to challenge the opponent. The covering defender is also responsible for preventing opponents from passing the ball through the space behind the first defender. The covering defender is like the free safety in American football, a player who is free to cover space and help teammates when needed. One or more players, the *third defender*(s), position diagonally behind the second defender to provide defensive balance. The third defender prevents opponents from passing the ball diagonally through the defense. Balance in defense protects the vulnerable space on the side of the field opposite the ball.

Responsibilities of the First Defender

The first defender applies direct pressure on the opponent with the ball. He or she positions goalside in proper defensive posture and attempts to do one of the following: (a) delay or contain the attacker until defending teammates can recover to positions goalside of the ball, or (b) force the attacker to dribble or pass the ball into an area where a covering defender can win the ball. The first defender should not attempt to tackle the ball until a covering teammate provides proper support (see Figure 8.1).

Responsibilities of the Second Defender

The second, or covering, defender(s) has two primary responsibilities. The first is to cover the space behind and beside the first defender. He or she must position to prevent a penetrating pass through that space and must also be ready to step forward to challenge an opponent who has beaten the first defender on the dribble. In most situations the second defender is also responsible for marking an opponent stationed

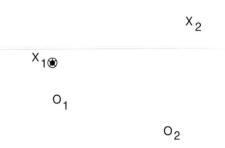

Figure 8.1 First defender applies pressure on the ball while second defender positions to cover space behind first defender.

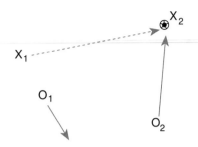

Figure 8.2 Proper angle of cover for the second defender. He or she protects space behind first defender and can also apply pressure to second attacker.

in the vicinity of the ball. To fulfill both obligations the second defender must position to protect the space behind the first defender and must also be able to challenge for the ball if it is passed to the opponent he or she is marking. Two important considerations are the angle and distance of cover.

The Angle of Cover

The second defender should position behind and to the side, not directly behind, the first defender where he or she can protect the space behind the first defender as well as mark an opposing player. He or she needs a clear view of the ball and must be able to readjust quickly to the attacker's movements (see Figure 8.2).

The Distance of Cover

Opponents must be denied time and space in the vital scoring zone front and center of your goal. The distance of cover should be reduced in that area of the field, but can be somewhat greater as the ball moves farther away from your goal. For example, if an attacker has the ball within 30 yards of your goal, the appropriate cover distance is approximately 2 to

3 yards, whereas 5 to 6 yards is appropriate when the ball is near midfield.

Remember that the second defender is also responsible for marking an opponent. The closer that opponent is to the ball, the tighter the cover. The distance of cover can be extended as the opponent moves farther from the ball (see Figure 8.3).

Responsibilities of the Third Defender

While the first defender is applying pressure at the point of attack and the second defender is providing cover, the third defender is responsible for providing balance. He or she should be positioned in the space behind the second defender along an imaginary diagonal line that begins at the ball and extends toward the goalpost farthest from the ball. From a position along the line of balance, the third defender can accomplish three important objectives: (a) protect the space behind the second defender, (b) keep the ball in view at all times, and (c) keep the opponent he or she is marking in view (see Figure 8.4).

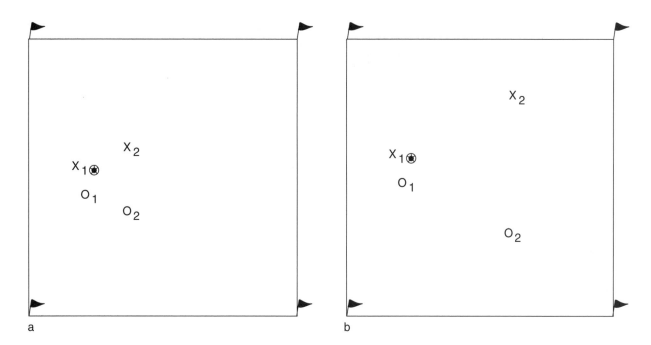

Figure 8.3 The distance of cover can change depending on whether the opponents are closer to the ball (a) or farther from the ball (b).

FIGURE 8.4 **KEYS TO SUCCESS**

GROUP DEFENSE

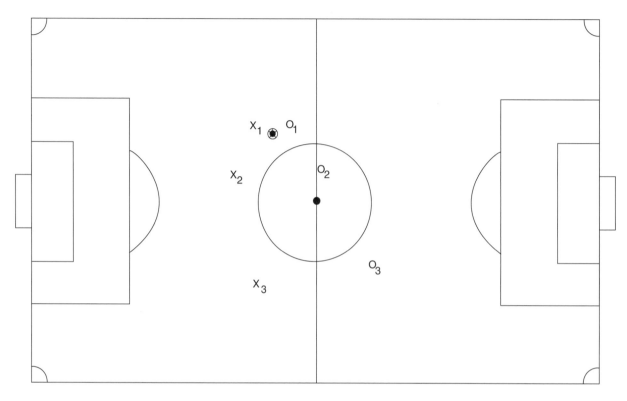

First Defender

1. Close distance to the opponent with the ball ___
2. Position yourself goalside in proper defensive posture ___
3. Maintain balance and control ___
4. Focus on the ball ___
5. Delay or contain dribbler's forward progress ___
6. Channel dribbler into restricted space ___
7. Channel dribbler into covering defender ___
8. Challenge for the ball ___
9. Win the ball ___
10. Initiate counterattack ___

Second Defender

1. Protect space behind first defender ___
2. Position yourself at proper angle in relation to first defender and ball ___
3. Position yourself at proper distance in relation to first defender and ball ___
4. Mark opponent in vicinity of ball ___
5. Keep ball and opponent in view ___
6. Intercept ball passed into space behind first defender ___
7. Assume role of first defender if he or she is beaten on the dribble ___
8. Assume role of first defender if ball is passed to the opponent you are marking ___

Third Defender

1. Protect space diagonally behind second defender ___
2. Position yourself along a line of balance extending toward the far goalpost ___
3. Keep the ball and nearby opponents in view ___
4. Readjust position along line of balance in response to ball movement ___
5. Intercept passes into the space behind the second defender ___

GROUP DEFENSE SUCCESS STOPPERS

Successful application of defensive pressure, cover, and balance requires coordinated movement by the first, second, and third defenders. Each player must read the situation correctly, anticipate the actions of his or her teammates, and react accordingly. Poor communication can lead to problems. Defensive breakdowns may also result if the first defender fails to contain the dribbler or if the second or third defenders position incorrectly.

Error	Correction
The First Defender	
1. The first defender attempts to tackle the ball and is beaten on the dribble before the second defender is properly positioned in cover.	1. You should not challenge for possession of the ball until a covering teammate supports you from behind. Instead, try to delay or contain the dribbler.
2. The first defender fails to apply immediate pressure at the point of attack.	2. You must put immediate pressure on the opponent with the ball. This action prevents a quick counterattack and also provides time for your defending teammates to recover to a position goalside of the ball.
The Second Defender	
1. The covering defender positions directly behind the first defender.	1. You will not be able to prevent an opponent's pass through the space beside the first defender if you position directly behind the first defender. Position at a diagonal from the ball in the space behind and to the side of the first defender.
2. The covering defender positions too far from the first defender.	2. When determining the proper distance of cover, you should consider the ability of the first defender, the area of the field, and the location of the opponent you are responsible for marking.
The Third Defender	
1. The third defender fails to protect the space behind the covering defender.	1. You should position diagonally behind the second defender along a line of balance extending toward the far goalpost. From there you will be able to keep the ball and nearby opponents in sight and also intercept a ball passed into the space behind the second defender. Keep in mind that the line of balance changes with the movement of the ball.
2. The third defender positions too close to the second defender and as a result is vulnerable to the long cross-field pass into the space behind him or her.	2. Don't be too concerned about providing close cover for the second defender. If the ball is played into the open space behind the second defender, you will have sufficient time to close the space while the ball is in flight.

GROUP DEFENSE

DRILLS

1. Two-Versus-Two Game

Play with three teammates; organize into teams of two players each. Use markers to outline a 15-by-25-yard field area and position a goal 4 yards wide at the center of each endline. Begin with a kickoff from the center of the field. Each team defends a goal. Score goals by kicking the ball through the opponent's goal below knee height. Do not use goalkeepers. Play for 20 minutes.

The primary emphasis in this drill should be on defensive pressure and cover. The first defender should apply immediate pressure at the point of attack; the second defender should position in cover to prevent the ball being kicked past the first defender through the goal. The second defender must also be in a position to challenge for the ball should it be passed to the opponent he or she is marking.

 **Success Goal** = Score more goals than opponents ___

Success Check
• Pressure at point of attack ___
• Proper distance and angle of cover ___

 To Increase Difficulty
(for Defenders)
• Require teams to defend two small goals on each endline.
• Make field larger to create more attacking space.

To Decrease Difficulty
(for Defenders)
• Make goals smaller.
• Reduce field size.

2. Two-Versus-Three Possession Game

Play with four teammates. You and one teammate form the defending team while the remaining players form an attacking team. Use markers to outline a 15-by-15-yard area. The attacking team attempts to keep the ball away from your team by passing, dribbling, or both within the grid. Award the attacking team two points each time it completes eight consecutive passes and one point for each pass completed that splits (goes between) you and your teammate. Award your team one point each time it wins possession of the ball or forces the opponents to play the ball outside of the field area. If your team wins the ball, immediately return it to the attacking team and continue the game. Play for 15 minutes and keep track of your score.

Success Goal = Score more points than opponents ___

Success Check
• Pressure on opponent with the ball ___
• Limit attacker's passing options ___
• Make play predictable ___
• Prevent the pass that splits the defenders ___

To Increase Difficulty
(for Defenders)
• Enlarge the playing area.

To Decrease Difficulty
(for Defenders)
• Reduce field area.
• Limit attackers to three or fewer touches to pass and receive the ball.

3. Three-Versus-Two (Plus One) Game

Organize into two teams of three players each. Play on a 20-by-30-yard field with a 4-yard-wide goal at the center of each endline. Award one team possession of the ball to begin.

The team with the ball attacks with three players while the opposing team defends with two players and a goalkeeper. The first defender should apply pressure on the opponent with the ball while the second defender positions to cover the space behind the first defender. If a defending player steals the ball, he or she must first pass it back to his or her goalkeeper before the team initiates an attack on the opponent's goal. The goalkeeper then moves forward to join his or her teammates in the attack. One member of the opponent's team quickly drops back into goal to play as a goalkeeper while his or her teammates assume the roles of first and second defenders.

Teams switch roles between attack and defense with each change of possession. Change of possession occurs when a defender steals the ball, when the goalkeeper makes a save, after a goal is scored, and when the ball leaves the playing field. Teammates alternate playing as the goalkeeper. Goals are scored by kicking the ball through the opponent's goal. Play nonstop for 15 minutes and keep track of your goals.

Success Goal = Allow fewer goals than opponents ___

Success Check
- Apply pressure at point of attack ___
- Prevent passes that split the defense ___
- Prevent penetration by dribbler ___

To Increase Difficulty

(for Defenders)
- Increase field size.
- Increase goal size.
- Add an extra attacker to create a four-versus-two situation.

To Decrease Difficulty

(for Defenders)
- Decrease field size.
- Decrease goal size.
- Limit attackers to three touches to play the ball.

4. Double Zone Soccer

Select nine field players and two goalkeepers to participate with you in this game. Use markers to outline a rectangular area of 35 by 50 yards, bisected by a midline. Place a portable regulation-size goal at each end of the field with a goalkeeper in each goal. Organize two teams of five field players each. Designate three players for each team as attackers and two as defenders. Station the attackers for each team in the opponent's half of the field and the defenders for each team in their own half. This creates a three-versus-two situation in each zone.

Each team defends its goal and can score in the opponent's goal. Attackers and defenders are restricted to movement within their assigned zone. A defender who steals the ball must pass it to one of his or her teammates in the opposite zone to initiate the counterattack; otherwise, regular soccer rules are in effect. The team scoring the most goals wins.

Success Goal = Score more goals than opponents ___

Success Check
- Apply defensive pressure at the point of attack ___
- Cover the most dangerous attacking space ___
- Prevent shots from area front and center of goal ___

To Increase Difficulty

(for Defenders)
- Increase field size.
- Do not use goalkeepers.
- Add an attacker to each team to make it four versus two in the defending zone.

To Decrease Difficulty

(for Defenders)
- Add a defender to each team to make it three versus three in each zone.
- Limit attackers to three or fewer touches to pass and receive the ball.

5. Four Versus Two (Plus Two)

Organize two teams of four players each. Use markers to outline a rectangular field area of 40 by 25 yards. Use cones or flags to represent two goals 5 yards wide positioned approximately 10 yards apart on each endline. Your team begins with the ball.

Each team must defend two goals and can score in either of the opponent's goals. The team with the ball attacks with four players; the opponents defend with two field players and a goalkeeper in each goal. If a defending player steals the ball, he or she must first pass it back to one of his or her goalkeepers before the team can counterattack. Teams switch from defense to attack and vice versa with each change of possession. Regular soccer rules apply except for the method of scoring. A team wins one point for eight consecutive passes without possession loss and two points for each goal. Play for 15 minutes and keep track of points.

Success Goal = Allow fewer points than opponents ___

Success Check
- Apply pressure at the point of attack ___
- Cover the most dangerous attacking space ___
- Force attackers to take shots from wide angles to goal ___

To Increase Difficulty

(for Defenders)
- Increase field size.
- Enlarge goals.

To Decrease Difficulty

(for Defenders)
- Make goals smaller.
- Reduce field size.
- Limit attackers to two touches to pass and receive the ball.

6. Three Versus Three (Plus One Neutral)

Divide into two teams of three players plus one neutral player. Use markers to outline a 30-by-30-yard playing area. Station both teams and the neutral player within the area. Use colored scrimmage vests to differentiate teams from each other and the neutral player. Award one team possession of the ball to begin.

The team with the ball tries to maintain possession. The neutral player always plays with the team in possession to create a one-player advantage for the attack. Change of possession occurs when a defending player steals the ball or when the ball goes out of play last touched by a member of the attacking team. Teams get one point for five consecutive passes without loss of possession and two points for eight or more consecutive passes. Play for 15 minutes. The team scoring the most points wins the game.

 **Success Goal** = Score the most points ___

Success Check
- Pressure on the ball by first defender ___
- Cover provided by second defender ___
- Balance provided by third defender ___

 To Increase Difficulty

(for Defenders)
- Increase size of playing area.
- Add a second neutral player to the game who also plays with the attacking team creating a two-player advantage for the attackers.

To Decrease Difficulty

(for Defenders)
- Restrict attackers to three or fewer touches to pass and receive the ball.
- Reduce the size of the playing area.

7. Half-Court Soccer

Organize into two teams of three players and one neutral goalkeeper. Play on one half of a soccer field with a regulation goal on the endline. Place a line of markers spanning the width of the field 30 yards from goal. Station one team (attackers) outside of the 30-yard zone with the ball. The other team (defenders) positions within the 30-yard zone. The neutral goalkeeper is in goal.

The attacking team enters the defending zone and tries to score in the regulation goal. Change of possession occurs when the ball goes out of play, when a foul occurs, when a goal is scored, when the goalkeeper saves a shot, or when a defender steals the ball. After each change of possession the ball must be passed outside of the 30-yard zone before a new attack on goal is initiated. Otherwise, regular soccer rules apply. Award two points for each goal and one point for a shot on goal saved by the goalkeeper. The team scoring the most points wins. Play for 25 minutes.

Success Goal = Score the most points ___

Success Check
- Apply defensive pressure at point of attack ___
- Position to ensure adequate cover and balance ___
- Quickly readjust defensive positions in relation to movement of the ball ___

 To Increase Difficulty

(for Defenders)
- Add a neutral player who always plays with the attacking team to create a one-player advantage for the attackers.

To Decrease Difficulty

(for Defenders)
- Limit attackers to three touches to control and play the ball.

8. Defending in a Numbers-Down Situation

Organize one team of five players and one numbers-down team of three players. Use markers to outline a field area of 30 by 40 yards. Position a goal 6 yards wide at the center of one endline. Position a small goal, 3 yards wide, at each corner of the opposite endline. Do not use goalkeepers. The team with five players defends the large goal and can score in either of the small goals. The other team defends the two small goals and can score in the large goal. The five-player team wins one point for each goal it scores. The numbers-down team wins two points for each goal it scores. Play for 10 minutes, then reorganize the teams with different players for the outnumbered team.

Success Goal = Score more points than opponents ___

Success Check
• Apply pressure at the point of attack ___
• Balance on the side of the field opposite the ball ___
• Prevent penetration via pass or dribble ___

To Increase Difficulty
(for Outnumbered Team)
• Increase size of goals the outnumbered team defends.
• Make the field wider.

To Decrease Difficulty
(for Outnumbered Team)
• Make the field narrower.
• Restrict the five-player team to three or fewer touches.

9. Game With Zonal Defense

Organize into two teams of five players each. Use markers to outline a 60-by-50-yard field. Position cones or flags to represent a regulation-size goal at the center of each endline of the field. Station a goalkeeper in each goal. Award one team possession of the ball.

Begin with a kickoff from the center of the field. Each team defends a goal and can score in the opponent's goal. Regular soccer rules apply. The only restriction is that each team must play a strict zonal defense. The defender nearest the ball applies pressure at the point of attack, nearby teammates provide cover, and defenders farthest from the ball position provide balance. Defending players must readjust their positions and responsibilities depending on the movement of the ball. Play for 30 minutes. The team conceding the fewest goals wins the game.

Success Goal = Score more goals than opponents ___

Success Check
• Coordinate defensive concepts of pressure, cover, and balance ___

To Increase Difficulty
(for Defenders)
• Add two neutral players to the game who always play with the attacking team to create a two-player advantage for attackers.

To Decrease Difficulty
(for Defenders)
• Limit team with ball possession to three or fewer touches.
• Add one neutral player to the game who always plays with the defending team.

SUCCESS SUMMARY

Depending on the situation you must be prepared to play the role of a first, second, or third defender. To establish a strong team defense, it is also essential that you understand how each role relates to the others. Communication with your teammates is important. For example, when playing as a covering defender you can verbally inform the pressuring defender to channel the attacker in a specific direction or cue him or her when to challenge for the ball. Ask your coach to observe you defend in small-group situations. He or she should pay special attention to the decisions you make when playing as the first, second, and third defender. Your coach can use the checklist in Figure 8.4 to rate your overall performance and provide feedback.

STEP

9

TEAM TACTICS: ATTACKING AND DEFENDING AS A UNIT

W hen a team is playing exceptionally well, each player seems to know in advance exactly what the others are going to do. Teammates move forward in unison, string together beautiful passing combinations, and create spectacular goal-scoring opportunities. It appears that 11 individuals are thinking with one common mind—and in a sense they are!

Team tactics channel the efforts of 11 teammates toward a common goal and help to put everyone on the same page, so to speak. Successful attack and defense are group projects, the result of the coordinated efforts of teammates, and can be accomplished only if all players have a clear understanding of the basic principles that underlie each.

Team Attack

Team-attack tactics create time and space, provide attacking players with a variety of options, generate numbers-up situations, and open up scoring opportunities. Keep in mind the important relationship between time and space on the soccer field—the more space available to you, the more time you will have to receive, control, pass, or shoot the ball.

Why Is Attacking as a Team Important?

The teamwork required to create and finish goal-scoring opportunities occurs when teammates are willing to mesh their talents and efforts for the common good. Your ability to choose the best course of action and to make the right decisions will in large part determine how much you contribute to your team's performance.

How to Attack as a Team

The following principles conceptualize the goals and objectives of team attack and provide a logical process for achieving them. Keep these guidelines in mind when your team has the ball.

Player Movement Without the Ball

Time motion studies demonstrate that the typical soccer player has possession of the ball for only 3 to 4 minutes during a 90-minute match. For more than 86 minutes, you will be without the ball! You must do more than just occupy space during that time.

There is an old saying among coaches that goes: "If you're going to stand and watch the game, buy a ticket." That may sound a bit harsh, but it's true. The team cannot afford a spectator on the field. Be in constant motion when your team has the ball. Your movements should be purposeful: to create space for yourself in which to receive a pass or to clear space for a teammate.

Use *diagonal runs* to penetrate diagonally through the opponent's defense. You can begin your run in the flank area and travel inward through the center of the defense, or you can begin from a central area and move toward the flank. In either case, diagonal runs have several advantages over runs that travel flat across the field. Diagonal runs penetrate into dangerous attacking space and force opponents to mark you, possibly drawing them into poor defensive positions. A diagonal run may also clear an area of opponents so a teammate can move forward into the open space. Finally, a diagonal run from the flank puts you in excellent position to penetrate and score should you receive the ball while moving through the defense (see Figure 9.1).

Use *checking runs* to create distance between you and the opponent marking you. If you recall, a checking run is a short, sudden burst of speed designed to fool the defender into thinking that you are going to run into the space behind him or her. Bluff a run forward past the defender, then suddenly check back toward the ball. Because the defender has been taught to maintain a position goalside of you, the distance between you and the marker increases when you suddenly stop and check back toward the ball. You can take advantage of the open space to receive the ball and turn to face the defender (see Figure 9.2).

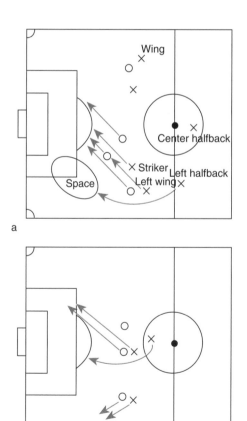

a

b

Figure 9.1 A diagonal run from flank (a) and a diagonal run from center (b).

Combination Play for Depth and Width

An attacking team that combines effective passing techniques with proper positioning of players forces the defending team to cover a larger field area. Passes should vary in type, distance, and direction and attackers should position themselves to provide *width* and *depth* to their team's system of play. This positioning of players, commonly referred to as the *proper attacking shape*, extends the attacking team vertically down the field and horizontally across the field.

You have learned that the player with the ball should have teammates in close support positions. A support player should position on each side and slightly ahead of the ball, and a third support player should position a few yards behind the ball. The function of the player behind the ball is to provide depth in the attack and to do what the player with the ball is not always able to do, that is, pass the ball forward. For example, if the player with the ball has his or her back to the opponent's goal, he or she can pass the ball back to the trailing player who can then pass it forward to an open teammate.

Your team can create space within the opposing team's defense by stretching itself vertically up and down the field. This is also an example of depth in attack—always position a minimum of one or two players well ahead of the ball for good depth. These front-running players spearhead the attack, playing as targets who receive and possess the ball until teammates can sprint forward in support.

Maintaining width in attack forces the defending team to cover a larger field area and can create gaps of open space within its defense. Flank players (*wingers*) positioned on the side of the field nearest the ball, and to some extent *weak-side players* positioned on the side of the field opposite the ball, provide width. Weak-side players are also in excellent position to make diagonal penetrating runs through the center of the opponent's defense (see Figure 9.3).

Improvisation—Tactical Use of Dribbling Skills

The intelligent use of dribbling skills is the best example of improvisation, or creativity, in attack. The player who has the ability to take on and beat opponents on the dribble can be the most dangerous weapon in a team's attacking arsenal. On the flip

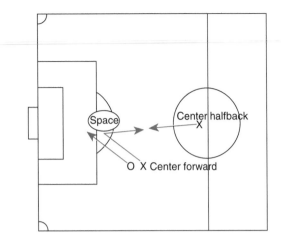

Figure 9.2 An example of a checking run.

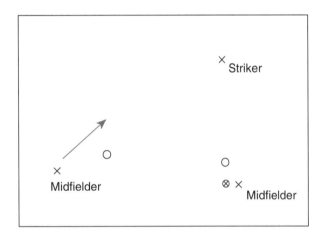

Figure 9.3 Width in attack: With the defense spread the weak-side midfielder makes penetrating run through defense.

side of the coin, excessive dribbling at inappropriate times or in the wrong area of the field quickly destroys the teamwork and continuity that produce an effective attack.

To clarify the tactical use of dribbling skills as they apply to different areas of the field, we can divide the playing field into three zones—the defending third, the midfield third, and the attacking third (see Figure 9.4).

Defending Third—Area of No Risk. Always weigh risk versus safety when choosing whether or not to take on an opponent. The defending third of the field nearest your goal is an area where you should take little or no risk. Do not attempt to beat an opponent on the dribble in the defending third where loss of possession may cost your team a goal. Rather than dribbling to advance the ball, it is much safer to pass the ball forward to an open teammate and then support your pass.

Midfield Third—Area of Moderate Risk. You can use dribbling skills with greater frequency and more positive results in the middle third of the field. If you beat an opponent on the dribble in this area, you can create a numbers-up situation as your team moves into the attacking third of the field. In the event you lose the ball on the dribble, you are still in position to recover and defend. Excessive use of dribbling skills in the midfield third is not warranted, however, because it tends to slow the attack and makes your play predictable.

Attacking Third—Area of Greatest Risk. You can use dribbling skills to best advantage in the attacking third of the field. The potential benefits of taking on an opponent in this area outweigh the risk of possession loss. If you can beat an opponent on the dribble in the attacking third, you may create an excellent scoring opportunity. In addition, loss of possession in this area will not pose an immediate threat to your own goal. Learn to recognize situations that warrant dribbling and take advantage of them. The result may be the ultimate aim of every attack—a goal.

Total Team Support

The concept of support can be generalized to the entire team if we consider each player as supporting a teammate and in turn being supported by one or more teammates. Soccer is sometimes called a game of triangles. This analogy refers to the support positioning of players as they move around the field area. If all 10 field players position themselves at the correct depth and angle of support with respect to nearby teammates, then the organization of players does resemble a series of interconnected triangles. These triangles are not static, however. Players must constantly readjust their positions based on the location of the ball and movement of teammates.

Total team support can be achieved only if teammates move up and down the field as a compact unit. As a general rule, there should be no more than 40 to 50 yards between the last defender in the back line and the deepest penetrating attacker in the front line (see Figure 9.5).

Figure 9.4 Risk and safety in the three sections of the field.

Create and Finish Scoring Opportunities

In a perfect world every attack would culminate in a goal. In the real world we know that just isn't possible. A team of determined opponents is doing everything within its power to prevent you from scoring. As a consequence, the individual who can consistently put the ball in the back of the opponent's net is an extremely valuable player. Success at scoring goals requires a combination of skill, determination, courage, and intelligent tactical play.

I've heard coaches say that great scorers are born, not made. They point out the intangible qualities that players like Romario of Brazil, Roberto Baggio of Italy, and Dennis Bergkamp of the Netherlands possess—qualities like anticipation, precise timing, great vision, composure under pressure, and the ability to be in the right place at the right time. It is no secret that certain individuals have more innate ability than others. But all players, regardless of inherent strengths and weaknesses, can improve their goal-scoring abilities through dedicated practice. Develop

your ability to shoot with power and accuracy. Learn to release your shot, or "pull the trigger," quickly and with either foot. Be able to recognize potential scoring opportunities and position yourself to best advantage.

Improving your shooting skills is not the only concern. You will still need the help and cooperation of others to score goals. You and your teammates must work together to create opportunities in the most dangerous scoring zones—the central areas of the field that provide a wide shooting angle to goal. Shots taken front and center of the goal are most likely to find the back of the net. Shots taken from the flank areas, where the shooting angle is reduced, will rarely beat a competent goalkeeper (see Figure 9.6).

Team Defense

You have already mastered the defending tactics used in individual and small-group situations. The next step is to incorporate all of these strategies into an overall plan for team defense.

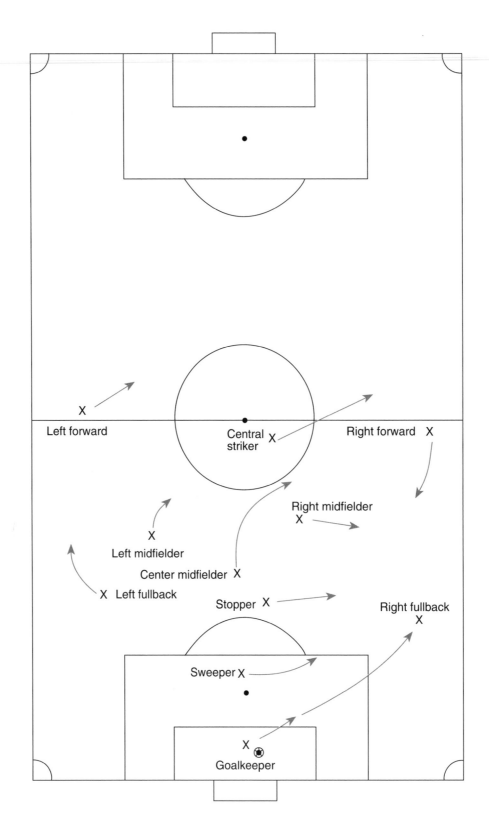

Figure 9.5 Total team support patterns.

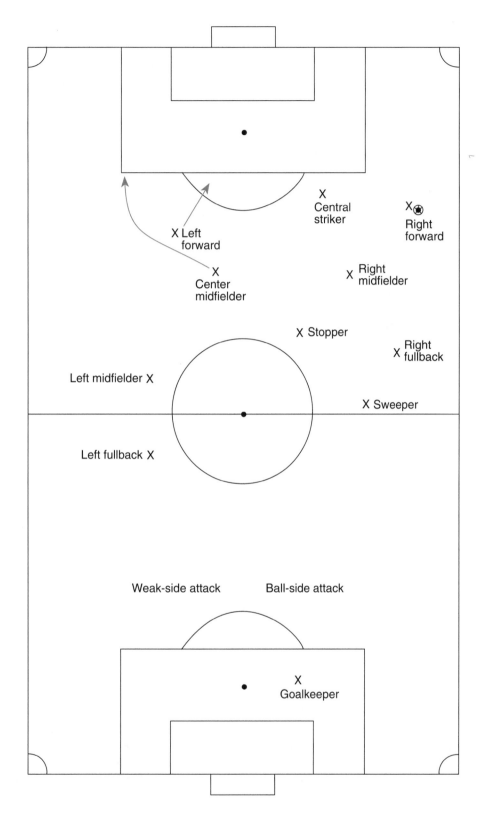

Figure 9.5 *(continued)*

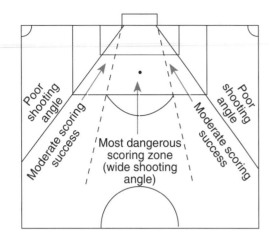

Figure 9.6 Scoring zones.

Why Is Defending as a Team Important?

Just as scoring goals depends on teamwork, so does successful team defense. A group of talented players will not necessarily form a cohesive defensive unit. Teammates must work together in an organized and disciplined manner to play team defense effectively.

How to Defend as a Team

The organization of a strong team defense depends on several factors. Players must be physically fit and play with a great deal of tenacity and determination. They must be able to compete successfully in one-versus-one situations. They must be strong in the air and able to outleap opponents to win air balls. Successful team defense also depends to a large extent on the decisions that players make in response to the changing situations that occur during play. Decisions such as when to challenge for the ball and where to position for optimal cover and balance affect the team's defensive efforts.

Poor decisions ultimately lead to poor team defense and goals scored against your team. You can improve your decision making by developing a clear understanding of what your team is trying to accomplish when the opponents have the ball. The following principles of team defense provide general guidelines on which to base your decisions. These prin-

ciples apply to all systems of play and progress through a logical sequence from the moment your team loses the ball until the instant it regains possession and goes on the attack.

Immediate Pressure at the Point of Attack

The defending team is most vulnerable to a counterattack during the few seconds immediately following loss of possession. Your teammates may be momentarily disorganized because they are in transition between attacking and defending modes of play. To prevent a swift counterattack and possible score, the defending player(s) nearest the ball must initiate an immediate challenge at the point of attack. The challenge should not be a reckless attempt to tackle the ball, but rather a calculated and controlled attempt to delay immediate penetration via the pass or dribble. If the pressuring defender can delay the opponent's counterattack for even a few moments, then his or her teammates will have extra time in which to regroup and organize their defense.

Recover Goalside and Delay

While pressure is applied at the point of attack, defenders away from the ball should quickly retreat to a position behind the ball. From a goalside position you will be able to keep the ball and the opponent you are marking in view and position to provide cover and balance for your teammates (see Figure 9.7).

Horizontal Compactness

The defending team's highest priority should be to eliminate the open space front and center of its goal, the area from where most goals are scored. Consolidating players in the most dangerous scoring zones has become an accepted tactic to achieve this objective.

Defending players should funnel inward toward the central area of the field as they retreat to a position goalside of the ball. They should also position to reduce the space available to attacking players in the vicinity of the ball. By compacting the defense horizontally, from side to side, defending players can eliminate open space within the defense and gain effective control of the most dangerous scoring areas (see Figure 9.8).

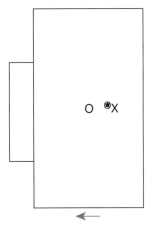

Figure 9.7 Goalside position.

Vertical Compactness

One or more teammates should provide cover, or depth, for the defender applying pressure at the point of attack. Depth in defense means to support from behind and also applies to the team as a whole. As defending players withdraw and consolidate in the most dangerous scoring zones, they must provide cover for one other. From a team perspective this is known as *vertical compactness.* Vertical compactness in defense reduces the open space between teammates and ensures that they are not aligned flat across the field. Failure to achieve vertical compactness leaves the defending team vulnerable to passes slotted diagonally through the defense (see Figure 9.9).

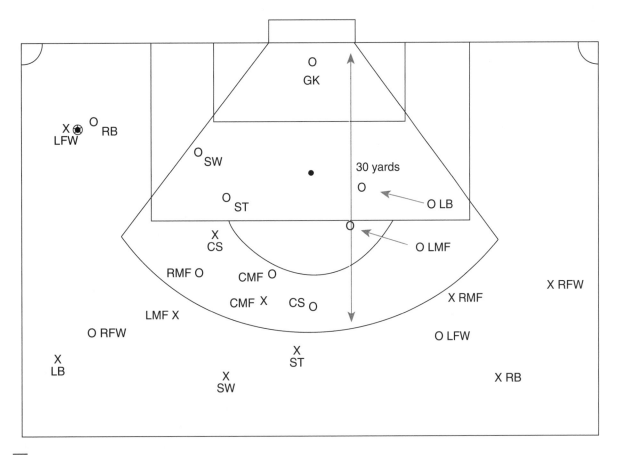

Figure 9.8 Compacting the defense.

Figure 9.9 Depth in defense.

Protect Space Behind the Defense

As defending players position themselves to reduce the space available within the defense, they must also position to protect the open space that exists behind the defense. According to the principle of defensive balance, players on the side of the field opposite the ball position along an imaginary diagonal line that begins at the ball and travels toward the far post of the goal. From there they can keep the ball and the opponent they are marking in view and also intercept an opponent's pass directed into the space behind the defense. As a general guideline, the farther a player is located from the ball, the deeper his or her position along the line of balance (see Figure 9.10).

Figure 9.10 Balance in defense.

The goalkeeper can also help to protect the open space behind the defense. He or she must be prepared to move forward from the goal area to cut off passes that enter the space behind the last defender. When the goalkeeper leaves the penalty area, he or she must play the ball with his or her feet.

Eliminate Passing Options

When defending players position themselves to reduce the open space within and behind the defense, they should also try to reduce the number of passing options available to the opponent with the ball. This can be accomplished in two ways. The first is by tight marking of all opponents stationed near the ball. The player with the ball will be forced to attempt a longer pass if nearby teammates are unavailable as passing options, and the chance of error is greater with a long pass. A second way to eliminate passing options is by positioning to block the passing lanes between attackers, thereby forcing the player with the ball to chip it over defenders or pass it square or back to a supporting teammate. In either case the advantage shifts to the defense. Lofted passes are more difficult to execute successfully than ground passes. Also, from a defensive perspective, a pass directed flat across the field or back toward the attacker's own goal provides additional time for defending players to organize and position to their best advantage.

Make Play Predictable

The goal of the attacking team is to maintain as many options as possible, to make it difficult for the defending team to anticipate what it is going to do. You can counter this tactic by making the play of the attacking team as predictable as possible. This principle is actually an extension of the previous one because, by reducing the number of passing options available to an opponent, you actually make his or her play more predictable. Once you know what an opponent won't do, you can better anticipate what that player will do in a given situation.

Another way to make play more predictable is to channel an attacker into an area where the space is limited. For example, when you force an opponent to dribble toward the sideline, you reduce the space through which he or she can pass the ball forward. In a sense you have limited the attacker's options and made play more predictable. You can achieve the same results by channeling an attacker into the space occupied by a covering teammate.

Win the Ball

We have discussed the principles of team defense in a methodical step-by-step progression, but actual implementation of these principles occurs swiftly and simultaneously. At this point the defending team should be in excellent position to win the ball. There is pressure at the point of attack, defending players are positioned to provide cover and balance for one another, the most dangerous scoring zones are protected, and the play of the attacking team has been made as predictable as possible. The final step in the sequence is to challenge for and win the ball.

TEAM TACTICS

DRILLS

Each of the following drills incorporates all of the principles of team attack and team defense. The coach or the players participating in the drill should choose the aspects of team attack and team defense they wish to emphasize in each particular situation.

1. Four-Goal Game

Play with 9 to 15 teammates divided into two equal-size teams. Use markers to outline a field area approximately 50 yards square. Place cones or flags to represent a small goal 4 yards wide on the center of each of the four sidelines. Begin the game with a kickoff from the center of the area.

Each team defends two goals and can score in two goals. Teams score by kicking the ball through either of the opponent's goals below waist height. Do not use goalkeepers. Regular soccer rules apply except that the offside law is waived. Play for 25 minutes and keep track of the goals scored.

Success Goal = Score more goals than opponents ___

Success Check
- Pressure, cover, and balance on the defense ___
- Width, depth, and penetration on the attack ___
- Quick transition from attack to defense and vice versa ___

To Increase Difficulty
- Add goalkeepers.
- Limit players to three touches to pass, receive, and shoot the ball.

2. Tight-Marking Game

Play with 9 to 15 teammates divided into two equal-size teams. Use markers to outline a field area of approximately 50 by 75 yards with a goal 4 yards wide at the center of each endline. Award one team possession of the ball to begin. Do not use goalkeepers. Begin with a kickoff from the center of the field.

Each team defends a goal. Require strict one-on-one marking of all players. Shots may be taken from anywhere on the field, so marking must be very tight to prevent long-range scores. Change of possession occurs when a defender steals the ball, when the ball goes out of play, or when a goal is scored. Play for 25 minutes and keep track of goals.

Success Goal = Score more goals than opponents ___

Success Check
- Defenders maintain goalside position ___
- Immediate pressure at point of attack ___
- Defensive cover and balance ___

To Increase Difficulty
- Limit players to three or fewer touches to pass, receive, and shoot the ball.

3. Game With Wingers

Divide into two teams of three players each plus two neutral players and two goalkeepers. Use markers to outline a rectangular playing area of 40 by 50 yards with a regulation-size goal at the center of each endline. Mark a zone 5 yards wide extending the length of the field on each flank. Station one neutral player (winger) in each flank zone and a goalkeeper in each goal. Begin the game with a kickoff from the center of the field.

Teams play three versus three in the central zone of the field. The neutral wingers join the team with the ball to create a two-player advantage for the attack. Wingers may move only within their flank zone. Goals can be scored directly from the central zone or from balls crossed into the goal area by the wingers. When a winger receives a pass from a central player or the goalkeeper, he or she must dribble to the defending team's endline and cross the ball into the goal area. Otherwise, regular soccer rules apply. Play for 25 minutes. Keep track of goals.

Success Goal = Score more goals than opponents ___

Success Check
• Maintain width and depth in attack ___
• Create scoring opportunities in central areas ___

To Increase Difficulty
• Restrict attacking team to three or fewer touches to pass, receive, or shoot the ball.
• Position a defending player in each flank zone to create a one-versus-one situation on the flank.

4. Three-Zone Game

Divide into three teams of three players each plus one neutral player, and two goalkeepers. Use markers to outline a playing area of 40 by 75 yards with a regulation goal on each endline. Divide the field into three equal 40-by-25-yard zones. Station a three-player team in each zone and a goalkeeper in each goal. The team in the middle zone begins with the ball. The neutral player always plays on the team in possession of the ball.

The team in the middle zone, assisted by the neutral player, attacks and attempts to score in one of the goals. The team defending the goal gains possession by tackling the ball or intercepting a pass, when the goalkeeper makes a save, when a goal is scored, or when the ball travels over the endline last touched by an attacking player. Upon gaining possession of the ball, the original defending team, along with the neutral player, moves forward into the middle zone and then attacks the opposite goal. The original attacking team remains in the end zone to play as defenders on the next shift. Regular soccer rules apply. Play for 25 minutes. Each team keeps track of its goals.

Success Goal = Score more goals than opponents ___

Success Check
• Defensive pressure at point of attack ___
• Cover and balance away from the ball ___
• Quick transition from defense to attack ___

To Increase Difficulty
• Limit attacking players to three or fewer touches to pass, receive, and shoot the ball.
• Add one additional player to each team to decrease the available space.

5. Game With Restricted Dribbling

Divide into two teams, each with five field players and a goalkeeper. Use markers to outline a rectangular area of 40 by 60 yards with a regulation goal on each endline. Divide the field lengthwise into three equal zones. Position a goalkeeper in each goal. Award one team the ball to begin.

Begin with a kickoff from the center of the field. Each team defends a goal and can score in the opponent's goal. Regular soccer rules apply, except for the following restrictions. In the defending zone nearest their goal, players may use one- and two-touch passing only. Players may advance the ball through the middle zone by passing or by dribbling into open space, but they may not take on and beat opponents in that area. Dribbling is mandatory in the attacking third of the field where players must beat an opponent by dribbling before shooting on goal. Violation of a zone restriction results in loss of possession to the opposing team. Play for 25 minutes and keep track of the score.

Success Goal = Score more goals than opponents ___

Success Check
- Think "safety first" in the defending third of the field ___
- Move the ball quickly through the midfield zone ___
- Create one-on-one situations in the attacking third of the field ___

To Increase Difficulty
- Add two players to each team to reduce the available space.

6. Pass, Dribble, or Shoot to Score

Organize two equal teams of five to eight players each plus goalkeepers. Use markers to outline a playing area of 50 by 70 yards with a regulation-size goal on each endline. Position cones or flags to represent a small goal 2 yards wide on each flank area near the midline. Station teams in opposite halves of the field and position a goalkeeper in each regulation-size goal. Begin with a kickoff from the center of the field.

Players have several scoring options. Award two team points for a goal scored in a regulation goal, one point for a pass completed to a teammate through a small goal on the midline, and one point for dribbling the ball over the opponent's endline. Play for 25 minutes and keep track of the points scored.

Success Goal = Score more points than opponents ___

Success Check
- Tight marking in vicinity of ball ___
- Pressure, cover, and balance in defense ___
- Width, depth, and combination play on attack ___

To Increase Difficulty
- Position four small goals along the midline.
- Limit players to three or fewer touches to pass, receive, and shoot the ball.

7. Six Versus Four

Designate a four-player team, a six-player team, and one goalkeeper. Use cones or flags to mark off an area of 50 by 70 yards. If a regulation field is available, play on one half of the field. Position a regulation goal on one endline and position two minigoals 20 yards apart on the other endline. Position the goalkeeper in the regulation goal; do not use goalkeepers in the minigoals. Award the six-player (attacking) team possession of the ball to begin the game. Designate the coach or an uninvolved teammate as the official scorekeeper.

The six-player team tries to score in the regulation goal, defends the minigoals, and earns points in the following manner:

- One point for eight passes in succession without loss of possession
- One point for a successful give and go (wall) pass
- One point for a shot on goal saved by the goalkeeper
- One additional point if the shot was taken from a central location—within the width of the penalty area
- Two points for each goal scored from within 18 yards of goal
- Two points for each goal scored off a ball crossed from the flank
- Three points for each goal scored when an attacker beats a defender on the dribble, shoots, and scores
- Three points for each goal scored from a distance of 20 yards or more from the goal

The four-player team earns one point for each of the following actions:

- Tackling (successfully) the ball
- Intercepting a pass
- Kicking the ball through either of the minigoals

Play for 30 minutes and keep track of your points on the scorecard on the next page.

Success Goal = Score more points than opponents ___

Success Check
- Execute all principles of team attack and team defense ___

To Increase Difficulty
- Place restrictions on players, such as limiting number of touches permitted to pass and receive the ball or requiring that all goals be scored off crosses.

Attacking Team Scorecard

8 passes in succession	_____ × 1 point = _____ points	
Successful give and go passes	_____ × 1 point = _____ points	
Shots on goal	_____ × 1 point = _____ points	
Shots from central location	_____ × 1 point = _____ points	
Goal scored within 18 yards	_____ × 2 points = _____ points	
Goals scored off crosses	_____ × 2 points = _____ points	
Goals scored by beating defender on dribble	_____ × 3 points = _____ points	
Goals scored from 20+ yards	_____ × 3 points = _____ points	
	Total = _____ points	

Defending Team Scorecard

Successful tackles	_____ × 1 point = _____ points	
Passes intercepted	_____ × 1 point = _____ points	
Goals in minigoals	_____ × 1 point = _____ points	
	Total = _____ points	

SUCCESS SUMMARY

Practice team tactics in competitive, matchlike situations. The games need not be full sided (11 players per team), but they must include a sufficient number of players so you can experience all the components of team attack and team defense. Meshing the individual parts (players) to form the team is the most difficult, yet most satisfying, aspect of playing soccer.

STEP
10
TEAM ORGANIZATION: SYSTEMS OF PLAY AND COMMUNICATION

A *system of play* refers to the collective organization of the 10 field players. The individual, small-group, and team tactics that you have learned to this point are universal to all systems, although player responsibilities and roles may differ from one system to another.

Several different systems of play were in use at the 1994 World Cup. Many teams, such as finalists Brazil and Italy, played with two forwards; others, like the Netherlands, played with three front-runners, and the United States, at times, played with only one forward. On defense some teams employed a traditional *sweeper*, but several played without a true sweeper in an alignment commonly called the *flat back four*. Some teams played strictly zonal defense; others utilized a combination of zone and one-on-one marking. None of these systems is inherently better than any other. They will all work if played correctly. Teams use different systems partly because of their overall philosophy of how the game should be played and partly because of the unique talents and abilities of their players.

Why Is Team Organization Important?

The system of play defines each player's role within the team. For example, two players may both be listed as *midfielders* but fulfill substantially different roles. One might be a defensive midfielder whose primary task is marking the opposing team's playmaker, whereas the other might be an attacking midfielder who creates scoring opportunities for his or her teammates. To achieve the teamwork necessary for successful team performance, each

player must understand his or her role within the team.

How Systems Are Organized

Ten field players and a goalkeeper make up a soccer team. Field players are usually designated as defenders, midfielders, and forwards. Variations in deployment of the field players result in different formations and player responsibilities.

A number of systems have come and gone throughout soccer's long history. Which system is best? It depends on the nature and ability of the players who make up the team. What works for your team might not be appropriate for another. The coach should implement a system that highlights player strengths and minimizes their weaknesses.

In describing a system of play, the first number refers to the defenders, the second to the midfielders, and the third to the forwards. The goalkeeper is not included in the numbering of players. The following discussion focuses on a few of the more popular systems of the modern era—the 4-2-4, the 4-4-2, the 4-3-3, and the 3-5-2—and also mentions a few new variations unveiled at the 1994 World Cup.

The 4-2-4 System

The 4-2-4 player alignment was first introduced during the 1958 World Cup by the Brazilian team. Blessed with a number of great players, including the incomparable Pele, the Brazilians captured the hearts and support of soccer fans around the world by winning the world championship. The 4-2-4 system gained widespread popularity as coaches at all levels of competition tried to emulate Brazil's success.

Four defenders are organized with a sweeper, one central (stopper) back, and right and left flank defenders. The flank (wing) defenders and stopper back generally undertake one-on-one marking responsibilities, and the sweeper provides cover for the other three defenders. The sweeper is generally designated as the "free" defender and is not assigned a specific opponent to mark.

Two midfield players, or linkmen, function as the connecting thread between the defenders and forwards. The midfielders must support their forwards on attack and must also provide a line of defense in front of the back line of defenders when the opposing team has the ball.

The forwards are organized with two flank players, or wingers, and two central forwards, or strikers. One striker usually stations deep in the opponent's defense as a target to spearhead the attack. The other striker generally plays more withdrawn where he or she can support the front-runner and help in the midfield as needed (see Figure 10.1).

The 4-4-2 System

Control of the midfield area is vital to team success. An obvious concern with the 4-2-4 system is the tremendous workload placed on the two midfielders. In an attempt to provide greater midfield control, some teams began to withdraw their wing forwards into the midfield to create a 4-4-2 alignment. Theoretically, a team with four players patrolling the midfield could dominate play in that area.

Player responsibilities in the 4-4-2 are similar to the 4-2-4. The four backs are aligned with a sweeper and three marking defenders. One midfielder patrols each flank while two position centrally. The strengths and abilities of the two central midfielders should complement one another: One usually plays an attacking role, and the other plays a more defensive role. There are no true wingers in the 4-4-2. The flank midfielders move forward and provide width in the attack when their team has possession of the ball. If the wing midfielders fail to make the quick transition from defense to attack, then the 4-4-2 takes on a defensive orientation (see Figure 10.2).

The 4-3-3 System

The 4-3-3 alignment is the product of efforts to create a balance between attack and defense while placing even greater emphasis on player mobility and interchanging of positions. The four defenders are organized in the same manner as the 4-4-2 system with a sweeper playing behind the two flank (wing) defenders and stopper back. The stopper back's task is to mark the opposing team's central striker,

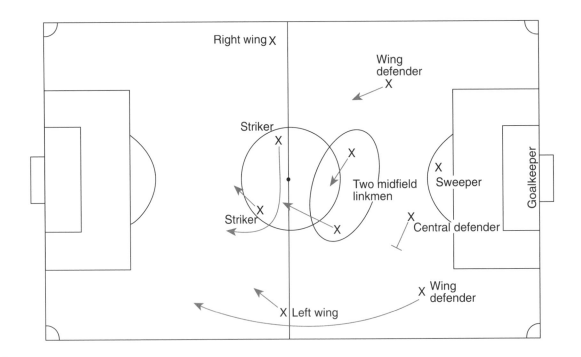

Figure 10.1 The 4-2-4 system.

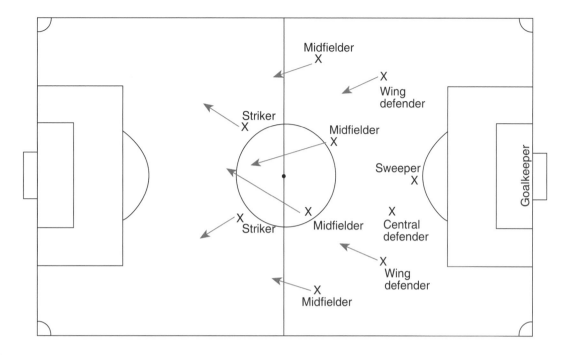

Figure 10.2 The 4-4-2 system.

whereas the flank defenders usually match wits with the opponent's wingers or flank midfielders.

The center midfielder is a key player in this system. He or she must be a creative playmaker, possess good passing and dribbling skills, and must also have the ability to move forward and score goals. On defense the center midfielder must be a strong tackler of the ball as well as a dominant player in the air. A wing midfielder flanks the center midfielder on each side.

Three forwards occupy front-running positions. A central striker spearheads the attack and is flanked on each side by a winger. The forwards must exhibit a great deal of movement both with and without the ball. Through intelligent off-the-ball running and interchanging of positions, they can confuse opponents and create space in which midfielders and defenders can move forward.

The 4-3-3 system requires that both midfielders and defenders contribute to their team's attack. This can be accomplished through the tactic of *overlapping runs*. At opportune moments defenders sprint forward from the back, overlap the teammate in front of them, and move into a more dangerous attacking position. If the run is properly executed, overlapping defenders and midfielders can catch the opponents by surprise and create dangerous scoring opportunities (see Figure 10.3).

The 3-5-2 System

A more recent development in the organization of players deploys three defenders, five midfielders, and two forwards. Germany used this system with great success during the 1986 and 1990 World Cups and many other teams quickly adopted it. The defense consists of a sweeper who plays behind two central markers. One midfielder generally assumes the role of the *windscreen*, or anchor player, who stations in front of the central defenders. Unlike the traditional defensive midfielder who marks a specific opponent, the windscreen plays in zonal coverage. His or her primary responsibility is to cover the other midfielders and prevent opponents from penetrating through the center of the defense via a pass or dribble. The remaining midfielders are usually deployed across the field, two centrally and one on each flank. Two forwards (strikers) spearhead the attack (see Figure 10.4).

New Systems of Play

The World Cup is often a showcase for the most up-to-date styles and systems of play. One of the most significant innovations at the 1994 World Cup was the greater reliance on zonal defense. Of the eight teams that advanced to the quarter finals of competition, only three—Germany, Bulgaria, and

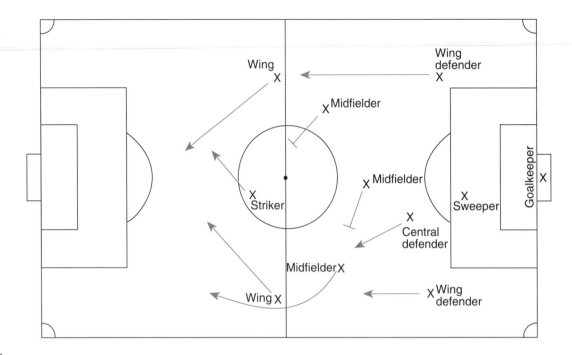

Figure 10.3 The 4-3-3 system.

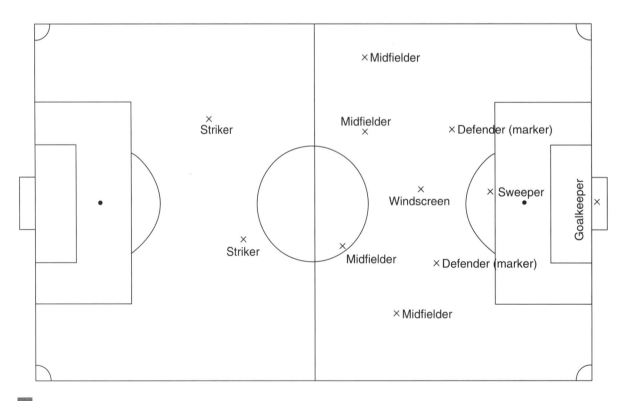

Figure 10.4 The 3-5-2 system.

Romania—played with a traditional sweeper and two central markers. Most teams deployed their defenders into the flat-back-four alignment. The four defenders organized zonally across the field do not have specific one-on-one marking responsibilities. The two central defenders provide cover for one another depending on who is pressuring the ball at any particular moment and shift their positions to provide cover for the flank defenders.

Most of the qualifying teams played either four or five players in the midfield with one or two players up front as targets. The Netherlands was the only team that consistently attacked with three forwards, although at times Bulgaria and Romania also played three up front. It is noteworthy that semifinalists Brazil, Sweden, and Italy all played the 4-4-2 system, yet did so in markedly different manners. Sweden displayed a defensive, counterattacking style of play, preferring to withdraw and concentrate defenders in its own end while trying to free its frontrunners via the quick counterattack. Brazil, on the other hand, played a much more open, attacking style with defenders and midfielders swarming forward to support the dangerous striking duo of Romario and Bebeto. Italy's version of the 4-4-2 fell somewhere between Sweden's defensive setup and Brazil's wide-open attacking game.

Signaling for Success

The soccer field is not a quiet place. It is usually filled with constant chatter as players communicate with one another during play. Your verbal commands can send important information to teammates and help them make wise game decisions. Follow these general guidelines when communicating with teammates:

1. Keep it simple—keep your comments clear, concise, and to the point.
2. Call early—provide your teammate(s) sufficient time to respond.
3. Call loud and clear—your teammate(s) doesn't have time to ask you to repeat what you said.

Teammates should adopt a standard set of verbal signals to avoid misunderstandings. The following commands are common in soccer and should be understood by all players.

When on the Attack

- Call "man on" when an opponent is directly behind a teammate who is receiving the ball. This will alert your teammate to shield the ball or receive the ball into the space away from the defender.
- Call "turn" to indicate that a teammate has sufficient space to turn with the ball to face the opponent's goal.
- Call "one touch" to inform your teammate not to stop the ball but rather pass it with his or her first touch.
- Call "one two" or "give and go" when you want your teammate to execute a wall pass.
- Call "hold the ball" to indicate that your teammate should protect (shield) the ball until supporting teammates arrive to help.
- Call "dummy it" when you want a teammate to let the ball roll past him or her to you.
- Call "switch it" to indicate a long cross-field pass to change the point of attack.

When on the Defense

- Call "mark up" to inform a teammate to use one-on-one marking.
- Call "step up" to instruct a teammate to reduce the space between himself or herself and the opponent with the ball.
- Call "close up" to instruct teammates to reduce the distance (space) between them, to position more compactly.
- Call "runner" to indicate that an opponent is running diagonally through or behind the defense.

In addition to verbal signals, you can use visual signals to communicate with teammates. Obvious signals include pointing to where you want the ball to be passed or where you want a teammate to move. You can also communicate with teammates in more subtle ways. A sudden glance in a specific direction or a slight nod of the head can alert teammates of your intentions. Since visual signals are often more difficult to interpret than verbal signals, they are generally used only by teammates who have played together on the same team for a period of time.

DRILLS

It is important to consider that a system of play is only a starting point and that once a game begins the alignment of players is in constant flux. In reality, if players adhere to the basic principles of team attack and defense, all systems end up looking alike during the course of play. The only real differences are the roles and responsibilities assigned to individual players. Consequently, there are no specific drills or exercises to practice the individual systems. However, you and your teammates can *shadow drill* to become familiar with the movement patterns of the various alignment systems.

1. Shadow Drill for Team Attack

Play on a regulation-size field with goals. Select the system to be used and position your teammates accordingly in one half of the field. Position your goalkeeper in the goal with a supply of soccer balls. The goalkeeper begins the exercise by distributing a ball to a defender or midfielder. From that point you and your teammates collectively pass the ball down the field and shoot it into the opposing goal. Do not involve any opponents in this exercise. Emphasize proper attacking movement of all players in relation to the movement of the ball as you pass it down the field toward the goal. After each score, players should return to their original positions. Repeat the exercise 15 times at half speed and 30 times at game speed or until all players feel comfortable with their role in the system.

Success Goal = 30 repetitions at game speed ___

Success Check
• Provide width and depth in attack ___
• Provide support for player with ball ___
• Readjust positioning in relation to movement of ball ___

To Increase Difficulty
• Limit players to two or fewer touches to pass, receive, or shoot the ball.
• Add six opponents who try to prevent your team from moving the ball the length of the field.

To Decrease Difficulty
• Slow speed of repetition.

2. Shadow Drill for Team Defense

Use same setup as the previous drill and add an opposing team to the exercise. Position your team to defend a goal while the opponents position in the opposite half of the field. The opponent's goalkeeper has the ball to begin.

The goalkeeper distributes the ball to one of his or her defenders. The opponents try to move the ball down the field to shoot at your goal. You and your teammates work together to prevent shots, gain possession of the ball, or both. The attacking team wins one point for each shot on your goal. After a shot on goal or if your team tackles the ball or intercepts a pass, immediately return the ball to the opposing goalkeeper. Repeat 30 times at game speed.

Success Goal = Concede 5 or fewer points to opponents ___

✔**Success Check**
• Pressure, cover, and balance on defense ___
• Horizontal and vertical compactness ___

To Increase Difficulty

(for Defenders)
• Use cones or flags to enlarge the defending team's goal.
• Require defending team to play with only eight field players.

To Decrease Difficulty

(for Defenders)
• Limit attacking team to three or fewer touches to pass, receive, and shoot the ball.

SUCCESS SUMMARY

Keep in mind that the perfect system of play does not exist; each variation is characterized by inherent strengths and weaknesses. It is the responsibility of the coach to select a system that best suits his or her team, a system that maximizes player strengths and minimizes their shortcomings. It is your responsibility to become familiar with the system of play, understand your role within it, and accept that role for the overall good of the group. Your opportunities for individual as well as team success will be greatly enhanced if you do.

RATING YOUR TOTAL PROGRESS

The following self-rating chart will help you judge your overall progress to this point. Read each item carefully and respond as objectively as possible. Rate your performance by writing a number in the space provided to the right of each soccer skill or tactic listed. After completing the inventory, assess your strengths and weaknesses, set new goals and objectives, and continue to improve your play.

Rating Points: 4 = outstanding, 3 = good, 2 = fair, 1 = poor

Fundamental Skills

Your first success goal in soccer is to develop the skills needed to play the game. Rate yourself on the following skills.

Passing Skills

Inside of foot ___
Outside of foot ___
Instep ___
Short chip ___
Long chip ___

Receiving Skills

Inside of foot ___
Outside of foot ___
Instep ___
Thigh ___
Chest ___
Head ___

Dribbling and Shielding Skills

Dribble for control ___
Dribble for speed ___
Shielding ___

Tackling Skills

Block tackle ___
Poke tackle ___
Slide tackle ___

Heading skills

Jump header ___
Dive header ___

Shooting Skills

Instep drive ___
Full volley ___
Half volley ___
Side volley ___
Swerve shot ___

Goalkeeping Skills

Goalkeeper stance ___
Receiving a rolling ball ___
Receiving a ball to side ___
Receiving a chest-high ball ___
Receiving a medium-high ball ___
Receiving a high ball ___
Diving ___
Distribute by rolling ___
Distribute by baseball throw ___
Distribute by javelin throw ___
Distribute by punting ___
Distribute by dropkick ___

Tactics

To improve your level of performance in soccer you must also understand and be able to execute the tactics used on an individual, group, and team basis. Rate your ability to use the following individual and group tactics in a game situation. Note: An assessment of team tactics is not listed since it depends on the group as a whole.

Individual Attack Tactics

Maintain ball possession ___
Create space for yourself ___
Turn on defender ___
Take on defender ___

Individual Defense Tactics

Goalside position ___
Approach to ball ___
Defensive posture ___
Marking distance ___
Containment ___
Preventing the turn ___
Tackle the ball ___

Group Attack Tactics

Give and go pass
  • First attacker ___
  • Wall player ___
Support positioning ___

Group Defense Tactics

First defender (pressure) ___
Second defender (cover) ___
Third defender (balance) ___

Overall Soccer Progress

Considering your competency in all of the skills and tactics listed previously, how would you rate your overall progress?

_____ Outstanding
_____ Pretty good
_____ Fair
_____ Needs work
_____ Needs a lot of work!

Glossary

Attacker: The player with possession of the ball. Front running attackers are usually called strikers or wingers.

Balance in Defense: Positioning of defensive players that provides depth and support. Players nearest the ball mark opponents while those away from the ball position to cover space.

Ball-Watching: As a defender, focusing solely on the ball and losing sight of the opponent being marked; a common error among inexperienced players.

Baseball Throw: A method used by goalkeepers to toss the ball over medium distances.

Blindside Run: A type of running off-the-ball in which a player without the ball runs outside of the opponent's field of vision in order to receive a pass.

Block Tackle: A defensive skill used to gain possession of the ball; the player uses the inside of the foot to block the ball away from an opponent.

Breakaway: Situation where an attacker with the ball breaks free of defenders and creates a 1 versus 1 situation with the goalkeeper.

Concentration in Defense: Positioning of defensive players to limit the space available to opponents in the most critical scoring areas.

Counterattack: The initiation of an attack on the opposing goal upon gaining possession of the ball.

Cover: Defensive support. As a defender challenges for possession of the ball he or she should be supported from behind (covered) by a teammate.

Cross: A pass originating from the wing or flank area that is driven across the goal mouth.

Defenders: A general term used to label the players positioned nearest to the goalkeeper. Most modern systems of play use four defenders.

Depth: Proper support positioning of the team, both in attack and defense.

Diagonal Run: Run designed to penetrate the defense while drawing defenders away from central positions.

Direct Kick: A free kick that can be scored without first touching another player.

Economical Training: Incorporating fitness, skill, and tactics into each drill or exercise to make maximal use of practice time.

Far Post: The goal post farthest from the ball.

Flanks: Areas of the field near the touchlines that provide a narrow shooting angle to goal.

Forwards: Players who occupy the front attacking positions; usually identified as strikers and wingers.

Full Volley: Striking the ball directly out of the air, most commonly with the instep of the foot.

Functional Training: Isolating for practice the techniques and tactics of specific player positions (such as the skill used by a striker in receiving the ball when under pressure of an opponent).

Give and Go Pass: A combination pass with one player passing to a nearby teammate and then sprinting forward to receive a return pass.

Goalside Position: Defending player positioned between his or her goal and the opponent to be marked.

Grid: A confined area in which a small group of players practices skills and tactics.

Half Volley: Striking the ball dropping from above the instant it contacts the ground.

Indirect Kick: A free kick from which a goal cannot be scored directly. The ball must be touched by another player before entering the goal.

Marking: Tight coverage of an opponent.

Mobility: Movement both with and without the ball designed to create space for teammates by drawing opponents into unfavorable positions.

Near Post: The goal post nearest the ball.

Offside Rule: A player must have two opponents, including the goalkeeper, between himself or herself and the opposing goal at the moment the ball is played. Otherwise, he or she is offside and is penalized by an indirect free kick awarded to the opposing team. Players cannot be offside if they are positioned in their own half of the field, if the ball was last played by an opponent, or if they receive the ball directly from a corner kick, throw-in, goal kick, or drop ball.

One-on-One Defense: System in which each player is responsible for marking a specific opponent.

One-Touch Passing: Interpassing among teammates without stopping the ball; also called first-time passing.

Overlap: Method in which a supporting teammate runs from behind to a position ahead of the player with the ball; often used as a tactic to move defenders and midfielders into attacking positions.

Poke Tackle: A method in which a player reaches in and uses the toes to poke the ball away from an opponent.

Ready Position: The goalkeeper's basic stance when the ball is within shooting range of the goal.

Restart: A method of initiating play after a stop in the action. Restarts include direct and indirect free kicks, throw-ins, corner kicks, goal kicks, and the drop ball.

Running Off-the-Ball: Movement of a player without the ball that creates passing and scoring opportunities for teammates.

Shielding: Positioning one's body between the opponent and the ball to maintain possession.

Shoulder Charge: A legal tactic used when challenging an opponent for the ball when the ball is within playing distance.

Slide Tackle: A method in which a player slides and kicks the ball away from an opponent.

Stopper Back: A central defender positioned in front of the sweeper back who usually marks the opposing center striker.

Striker: A front-running forward positioned in the central area of the field; usually one of the primary goal scorers on the team.

Support: Movement of players into positions that provide passing options for the teammate with the ball.

Sweeper Back: The last field player in defense who provides cover for the marking defenders.

System of Play: Organization and responsibilities of the 10 field players.

Tactics: Organizational concept on an individual, group, or team basis of player roles within the team structure.

Techniques: Game skills which include passing and receiving, heading, dribbling, shooting, and shielding.

Throw-In: A method of restarting play after the ball has traveled outside the touchlines. The ball must be held with two hands and released directly over the head. Both feet must be touching the ground when the ball is released.

Touchline: A side boundary line.

Two-Touch Passing: Type of interpassing in which the receiving player controls the ball with the first touch and passes to a teammate on the second.

Wall Pass: A combination pass with one player serving as a barrier to redirect the path of the ball. The player in possession passes off the "wall" and immediately sprints forward into open space to receive the return pass.

Width in Attack: Using the width of the field in an attempt to draw defending players away from central positions. The objective is to create space in the most dangerous attacking zones.

Wingbacks: Defenders positioned on the flanks who usually mark the opposing wing forwards.

Winger: A front-running forward positioned in the flank area near the touchline.

Zonal Defense: System in which each player is responsible for defending a certain area of the field.

ABOUT THE AUTHOR

Joe Luxbacher has more than 30 years of experience playing and coaching soccer at all levels. A former professional soccer player for the North American Soccer League, American Soccer League, and Major Indoor Soccer League, Joe is head soccer coach at the University of Pittsburgh, a position he has held since 1984.

Widely respected by soccer coaches and players alike, Joe holds an "A" coaching license from the United States Soccer Federation. He was named Big East Athletic Conference Coach of the Year in 1992 and 1995, and was selected for the Beading Soccer Club Hall of Fame in 1995. Joe, the author of nine books and more than 70 magazine articles on sport and fitness-related topics, serves as the fitness editor of *Total Health Magazine*.

Joe earned his PhD from the University of Pittsburgh in 1985 with a specialization in physical education and management and administration of athletics. Since 1978 he has served as the director and president of Keystone Soccer Kamps, helping hundreds of young people each year master the fundamentals of the game. He also directs the Shoot to Score soccer camps that focus on the skills and tactics needed to score goals.

Joe and his wife, Gail Ann, live in Pittsburgh, where they enjoy traveling, hiking, bicycling, and outdoor photography.

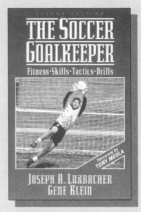
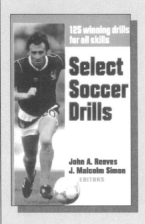